America's

Lost

Morality

Jim Booth

2012

Author's note:

There are several sections in *America's Lost Morality*, which may still be subject to court decisions at the time of writing. Any comments made on these cases were valid as at 12 July 2012.

Contents

Introduction   1

Part I. – Lost Morality in American Culture   **9**

1   Immorality of American Gun Culture   11
2   Sanctity of Life   24
3   Climate Change   32
4   Racism   39

Part II. – Lost Morality in Big Business   **45**

5   Wall $treet   47
6   The Subprime Mortgage Crisis   52
7   Big Oil & Gas   60
8   Corporate Environmental Disasters   67
9   Big Pharmaceuticals and Corruption in the FDA   74
10   Big Tobacco   84
11   Dying for Fast Food   89
12   Sins of Monsanto   96
13   Non-GM based Agriculture   106
14   People vs Profit   117
15   Disgraceful Executive Salaries   129
16   The End of Capitalism?   139

Part III. – Lost Morality in Government   **147**
          Foreign Affairs

17   The Middle East   149
18   War, Torture and Rendition   156

Part IV. –Lost Morality in Government   **167**
       Domestic and Judicial

19	American Tea Party	169
20	Donations, Lobbying and Political Corruption	179
21	Politics and Religion	183
22	The CIA – Ethics and Morality	190
23	The Patriot Act	198
24	The Judicial System	202
25	Moral Questions of the Bush Administration	209

V.   **The Final Chapter**   **215**

26	Is America's Morality Lost Forever?	217

Appendices   223

Notes   227

America's
Lost
Morality

Introduction

∞∞∞∞

In the beginning

In its relatively short history, the United States has evolved to become the world's largest economy and superpower. It has achieved this largely from its sense of self-belief, its capacity for innovation and the foresight of its founding fathers. In the last 100 years, the American people have developed the concept of the production line through Henry Ford; created the aviation industry through the determination of the Wright Brothers; have put man on the moon; pioneered and developed the computer industry and countless other notable achievements. Americans are rightfully proud of their country and its current place in history. The question *America's Lost Morality* asks is, to what degree was this success based on moral values and how have they changed over the past few decades?

There is a deep seated cultural belief in the United States that America is a highly ethical society, which sets an example for the rest of the world. This belief emanates from their early Christian heritage and has become ingrained as an integral part of the American psyche.

It is a widely accepted view of most religious adherents that the central core of moral standards can be traced back to the original Scriptures of their respective religions. This is particularly true with the three Abrahamic religions, Judaism, Christianity and Islam. Whilst some secularists might even agree with the view that human ethics has its genesis in supernatural revelation, most believe that the true source of ethical standards and behaviour stem from human facilities such as logic, reasoning or moral intuition.[1] Regardless of one's belief, the United States is arguably one of the Western world's most religious countries.

The US Census doesn't ask about religion, but according to one survey, 78.4% of Americans consider themselves to be Christian.[2] Furthermore, Gallup International indicates that 41% of Americans attend regular religious services.[3] This is considerably higher than France with 15% attendance, United Kingdom with 10%,[4] and Australia with just 7.5%.[5] Given the strength of religious conviction in the United States, it is easy to understand why there has always been a cultural philosophy of moral self-righteousness for over 200 years. This philosophy was destined to become the cornerstone of American exceptionalism.

Many believe that American exceptionalism can be traced back to its Puritan Roots,[6] which embraced the belief that God made a covenant with their people and had chosen them to lead other nations of the Earth. One Puritan leader, John Winthrop suggested that the Puritan community of New England should serve as a model community for the rest of the world.[7]

The French Writer, Alexis de Tocqueville, first described American exceptionalism, in his 1831 work, *Democracy in America.*

> The position of the Americans is therefore quite exceptional, and it may be believed that no democratic people will ever be placed in a similar one....Let us cease, then, to view all democratic nations under the example of the American people.

Unfortunately, many neo-conservative writers have aligned American exceptionalism with the implication of superiority. Herman Cain, who was a candidate for the Republican Party nomination for the 2012 presidential election, stated in an article entitled: *In Defense of American Exceptionalism:*

> There is no denying it: America is the greatest country in the world. We are blessed with unparalleled freedoms and boundless prosperity that for generations have inspired an innovative and industrious people. America is exceptional.[8]

It is clear that this statement is made by a man who is a proud American and it is a view that would be shared by many, if not most of his fellow citizens. But Cain goes on to say:

> American Exceptionalism is the standard that our laws reflect the understanding that we are afforded certain

God-given rights that can never be taken away. We know that God, not government, bestows upon us these inalienable rights, and because of that, they must not be compromised by the whims of man.

Here we see the beginnings of a divergence from the micro-level morality of the largely Christian public and the macro-level justification for political and economic business decisions, based on a "God-given right", regardless of the consequences of these decisions. So just how do these micro and macro level belief systems differ? First, let us examine the primary function of most religious institutions, with regard to ethics and moral standards.

At the micro or individual level, people are taught the basic tenets of what is right and what is wrong. For example, most individuals accept that it is wrong to harm other people, physically, emotionally or financially. This is exemplified by the Golden Rule "Do unto others as you would have them do unto you."

There can be no doubt that religion provides guidelines to their followers and support for those who need it most. So how can it be that the same people, who so strongly believe in these cultural, religious and moral values, can often ignore their fundamental tenets, once they reach a position of power? The answer it seems is that they can justify their decisions, no matter how far they deviate from accepted moral standards, by simply saying, "We have a God-given right." When this belief becomes the holy mantra of the military, politicians and doyens of big business, then decisions are made, which inevitably contribute to *America's Lost Morality*.

4

How morality has changed

It is clear that this micro-level morality justifies any measures the country may take to enforce its political ideology on others. At a macro level, however, morality is almost non-existent. This is, in part, due to politicians at the highest levels being corrupted by political lobbyists from large corporate enterprises. These include; Big Pharmaceuticals, Big Oil, Big Tobacco, Wall Street and many others. There is also a serious question mark over the objectivity of the politically-biased Supreme Court and their role in the decline of America's morality. The extent of these unethical relationships between business, government and the judiciary has affected the general public and the global perception of the United States, is the primary focus of *America's Lost Morality*.

Many decisions which have been made by the highest echelons of power have had dire consequences for Americans at home, as well as for millions of people around the globe. The massive monetary and humanitarian cost of some of these decisions cannot be ignored.

The book also focuses on the moral failure of both political parties, where wars have been illegally waged on other sovereign nations and justified solely on ideological grounds. In the past, there has been a sense that God has given them the right to impose American ideals on the rest of the world, but at what cost? The answers are quite disturbing.

The role that United States has played in the United Nations and the disastrous outcomes of many of its decisions, particularly in relation to the Israeli – Palestinian conflict is questioned in this book. America has always believed that their position in this conflict is morally justified, even though in many cases, they were at odds with the rest of the world.

As well, *America's Lost Morality* analyses domestic and world opinion on many controversial subjects of ethical importance, including; gun control, abortion, euthanasia, human cloning and the death penalty. It also questions the perceived morality of the Tea Party movement, sponsored mainly by the religious right. Tea Party advocates espouse the idea of getting America back to their moral and ethical past. However, when one takes a closer look at some of the backers of this movement, it is clear that all is not what it seems. The book explores the reasons behind the creation of the Tea Party and what the real ramifications of its philosophies are, from a moral and ethical perspective.

Finally *America's Lost Morality* examines the disastrous effects that this moral duality has had on the environment. One can only hope that as a result of America's actions at home and abroad, that the world has not been pushed past the yet-to-be determined environmental tipping point. Unless the decision-makers are prepared to make supreme personal, ideological and egotistical sacrifices, then the future for America's children and grandchildren appears to be very bleak indeed. Sadly, the effects of the high moral ground taken by the US government, its business leaders and its military is not confined to just the American people. Decisions made by those in power affect all of us, regardless of where we live.

It is often argued that America's esteem has suffered irrefutable damage in the eyes of the rest of the world, largely as a result of the decline in ethical values over the past several decades. *America's Lost Morality* asks the question, is it too late for the United States to turn this perception around?

America's Lost Morality

Part I

Lost Morality in American Culture

America's Lost Morality

Chapter 1

The Immorality of American Gun Culture

∞∞∞∞

The 2nd of April 2012 started off like any other day at the Oikos University in East Oakland, California. The college caters to the Korean American Christian community offering degrees in theology, music, nursing and Asian medicine. By the end of day, a shooting spree at this little known college left seven people dead and three wounded. Jean Quan, the Oakland Mayor summed up the tragedy by stating;

> "No American mayor wants to have this situation," she said. "It seems over the last decade, we've gotten used to seeing senseless mass killings like this, and we'll have to question the availability of guns and the need for other services in our community."[9]

Jean Quan is right to question gun availability in the United States. But is anybody listening? Is the gun culture so ingrained in the American psyche that the massive action necessary to change this culture is highly improbable, if not impossible. The real problem is that most people in the United States seem to support their constitutional right to bear arms, in spite of all these killings. How else could one justify the fact that 88% of Americans own guns?[10] The question is, do these people own guns because of their love of the constitution or do they own them out of fear? Perhaps they just accept it as the right thing to do. This would not be surprising given the constant barrage of gun-related violence as being justified in many TV shows and Hollywood movies. My own personal observation may be symptomatic of how the gun culture in America keeps on persisting to this present day.

When I was young, I was always impressed with the magic of Hollywood movies where we watched with great anticipation as to how superheros and western cowboys would defeat their adversaries. At the same time, TV brought us copious series of police dramas, which were also about good vs evil. Whether it was at the movies or sitting at home watching television, we were always delighted when the bad guys were caught and placed behind bars. But it was many years later that I realised what I was really witnessing. According to American folklore, as depicted in the movies and TV dramas, the good always defeated evil through violence – and in most cases, guns were the source of that violence.

I often reflected on this fact and wondered how much of this was as a result of the accepted gun culture in America based on the Second Amendment. Is it possible that Hollywood fiction could have been inadvertently used to indoctrinate its viewers at a young age? Or is it more likely that the filmmakers already accepted a gun culture as their constitutional right and simply used this as a justifiable background for their films?

In an attempt to seek answers to these very complex questions, we need to go back over 200 years ago, to when it all started. On 15th December 1791, the Second Amendment to the United States Constitution, a part of the United States Bill of Rights, was adopted along with the rest of the Bill of Rights. In part, this amendment protects the right of the people to keep and bear arms. A little over 200 years later, this right has grown into a culture of violence, unprecedented in the civilised world. The statistics, which should send alarm bells ringing to any individual or politician, are staggering to say the least. Yet somehow, thanks to powerful lobby groups such as the National Rifle Association, certain State laws and recent court decisions, the immorality and the accompanying violence of gun ownership, looks set to continue for the foreseeable future.

Amongst gun owner advocates, one can often hear the well quoted mantra that "guns don't kill people, people kill people". On the surface, this argument appears to have some merit. The problem occurs when people use guns to kill others, yet seem to be protected by their "constitutional rights" and lax interpretation of State laws. An example might be when a gun is used in so-called self-defence, even if the supposed assailant is unarmed.

One instance of such an event occurred on 26th February 2012, when George Zimmerman, a white 28 year old member of Neighbourhood Watch and a resident of a gated community in Florida, shot and killed an unarmed 17 year-old youth, Trayvon Martin,[11] for no apparent reason other than he was black and wearing a hoodie. Zimmerman claims that he shot him in self-defence, but how could this be? When Zimmerman called emergency operators after spotting a suspicious looking black male in the neighbourhood, he was given very sound advice not to pursue Martin. However, Zimmerman ignored this directive and pursued Martin with only one purpose in mind and that was to kill him, knowing that he may well be protected under his rights as stated in the Second Amendment.

What made this story even more bizarre, particularly to non-Americans, was that the Florida attorney's office, headed by Norman Wolfinger, determined that there wasn't enough evidence to lead to a conviction.[12] This is not to say that events like this could not have happened in countries like Canada or Australia. They do and that is a fact of life. However, in these countries, the perpetrator, namely George Zimmerman, would have at least been charged immediately with murder or manslaughter. Then it would be up to a jury to decide his fate. This is the only approach that is morally correct. Interestingly, neither of these countries have an equivalent of the "Second Amendment" to fall back onto. Perhaps, if they had had one, it would have been scrapped early in the twentieth century on moral grounds alone. Fortunately, after much protest throughout the United States, common sense prevailed and Zimmerman was finally arrested. Time will tell whether moral justice will be served.

In a related incident, Marissa Alexander had been threatened by her husband and she fired a warning shot to scare him off, as she desperately feared for her own safety. Her husband had a history of violence and even beat her while she was pregnant. Yet this incident, which happened in 2010, also in the State of Florida, made the headlines for all the wrong reasons.

14

Alexander was found guilty of 3 counts of aggravated assault and sentenced to 20 years imprisonment.[13] So how can this possibly be? One man, who is minding his own business, is shot and killed by someone, who had no right to be there and the killer is not even arrested until there was such a public outcry, the State of Florida had to respond to protect its image. The other case involves a lady who feels threatened by her violent husband and she fires a single round to scare him off and gets 20 years.

Can anyone make sense of these ridiculous laws? In Afghanistan, if a woman is raped, she can be stoned to death under Sharia law, while the perpetrator does not even get so much as a fine. How are decisions like these any different? Until the United States laws stop punishing the victims and letting the aggressors off, then they will be viewed by many as no better than the Afghan Sharia laws.

Congresswoman Corinne Brown stated outside the courthouse, after the sentence was handed down;

> "The Florida criminal justice system has sent two clear messages today," Brown said afterward. "One is that if women who are victims of domestic violence try to protect themselves, the `Stand Your Ground Law' will not apply to them. ... The second message is that if you are black, the system will treat you differently."[14]

Much of the problem is as a result of "Stand Your Ground" laws, adopted in 21 states, which allowed Zimmerman to walk free. The law, supported by the National Rifle Association and introduced by Jeb Bush, when he was governor of Florida, extends the right to use lethal force in self-defence from the home into the public domain.[15] Interestingly, the number of "justifiable homicides" has almost tripled since the law was introduced in 2005.[16] This is an extremely grey area and one wonders what the outcome may have been if Zimmerman was black and Trayvon Martin was white.

Another problem with excessive gun ownership seems to be exacerbated when there is such a fine line between what is deemed free speech and what is morally correct, especially when the free speech comes from a political identity. A case in point is the following story, which made worldwide headlines:

> In January last year (2011) in Arizona, Congresswoman Gabrielle Giffords was shot, among 18 people, six of whom died. The previous year, former vice-presidential candidate Sarah Palin had posted a map with the cross-hair symbols of a gun scope on the states that had Democrats running for re-election. Ms Giffords was among those listed below the map.[17]

While it is agreed that Palin did not commit a crime, her misguided use of what some would refer to as violent language, goes a long way towards perpetuating the gun culture in the United States.

Admittedly, the rights or wrongs of gun ownership cannot be summed up through an isolated incident. This was the sentiment of Bob Templeton, head of the Tucson Crossroads of the West Gun Show, where during an interview with ABC Australian television in March 2011,[18] he stated;

"...180 million gun owners in America. We have one guy, who went off the rails in an act of violence like he did. Should 180 million gun owners, who use guns lawfully in their regular activity be penalised for a mentally ill person, who clearly had an agenda and who perpetrated one of the most heinous crimes we ever seen?"

On the surface, this seemed like a legitimate question. But the facts are substantially different to what Templeton was implying. The truth is that this was not an isolated incident. In the same program, Michael Bloomberg, Mayor of New York City, offered the following comment;

"...34. That is the average number of Americans murdered with guns every single day." He also stated: "If you have a driver's licence, you can buy a 9mm gun at the Tucson gun show in the time it takes to buy a hamburger at McDonalds."

The total of 34 daily gun killings is a disgrace in its own right, but it only tells part of the story. When one takes the number of suicides and accidental deaths into account, the number of gun-related deaths per day in the United States, rises to 85.[19] That is more than three people every hour, dying from gun-related injuries. In spite of Bob Templeton's feeble attempt to describe the Gifford case as an isolated event, these figures clearly indicate that the American gun culture is seriously flawed and highly immoral. So how does America compare with other developed nations? In the next table, we compare the total deaths by guns per 100,000 people in each country. Here are a few examples:

United States	10.27
Switzerland	6.40
Canada	4.78
Australia	2.94
Spain	.90
Japan	.07

A complete list can be found in Appendix A.[20] It is clear that the United States is out of step with much of the civilised world. This is further supported by another table showing the largest civilian arsenals for each of 178 countries. (Refer to endnote.)[21] It comes as no surprise that the United States heads the table with 88.8 firearms per 100 people. Below is a comparison of the same six countries listed above.

United States	88.8
Switzerland	45.7
Canada	30.0
Australia	15.0
Spain	10.4
Japan	.6

As you can see, in most instances, the countries with the least amount of guns have the fewest number gun-related deaths. This is clearly illustrated in the graph below, which combines the two tables above. There should be absolutely no doubt in anyone's mind that if the United States is serious about reducing gun-related deaths, then the first step is to drastically reduce the number of guns in the community.

Fig. 1.1 (Death rate to Gun Ownership rate)

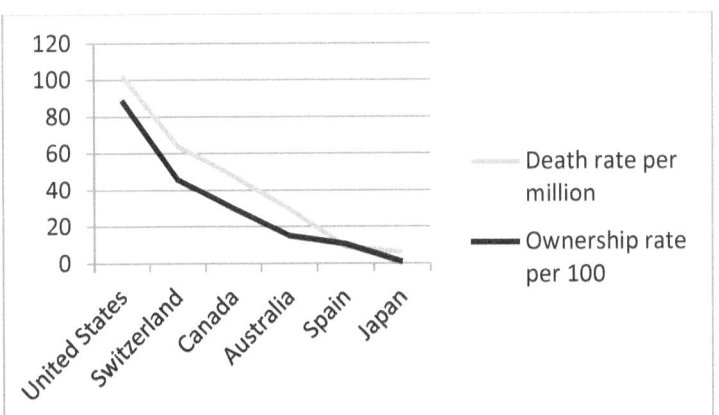

This is further supported by what has happened in Australia since tougher gun ownership laws were introduced in 1996. Fig 1.2 below shows how gun-related deaths changed in Australia.[22]

Fig. 1.2 (Gun-related deaths before and after gun control)

Australian gun-related deaths	1996 Before Gun Control	2008 After Gun Control
Gun-related homicides	104	19
Gun-related suicides	382	170
Gun-related accidental deaths	30	5

The United States has approximately 14 times the population of Australia. If we were to extrapolate the 2008 figures above, after gun control was introduced, to the United States, the resultant figures would be staggering.

Fig. 1.3 (Projected gun-related deaths in US with gun control)

US gun-related deaths	2010^{23} Actual	With Gun Control
Gun-related homicides	11,015	266
Gun-related suicides	19,308	2,380
Gun-related accidental deaths	600	70

It needs to be stated that the Australian figures in 1996 were starting from a low base. This is because gun ownership per capita is six times lower than it is in the United States. Nevertheless, up to a staggering 28,000 fewer deaths per year are possible, should the United States have the courage to introduce gun control measures, similar to those which were introduced in Australia in 1996.

These figures are proof positive that gun control works. Yet, one of the prime movers in the Tea Party, a former Arizona sheriff named Richard Mack, does not see it that way. Whilst giving a speech at a Tea Party meeting, he made the following statement;

"One thing we know about gun control is that it has never provided security, safety, freedom or peace – EVER." In an interview with an Australian reporter, Mack also said: "It's irrational to punish the innocent for the acts of the guilty."[24]

In a further insight to the Arizona gun culture, Gabriel Chin, a Law Professor at Arizona University, stated;

"People should be allowed to have guns. People should be encouraged to have guns. That's the type of State we are"[25]

Charles Hiller, who hosts a radio show called, *America Armed and Free* stated;

"Firearms are a symbol of freedom. Free men and free women own guns and subjects do not."[26]

Hiller is obviously unaware that Australia, Canada, Spain and Japan are all free countries and the figures above clearly dispute his rhetoric.

These examples show just how much the role of indoctrination plays in the support of the Arizona gun laws. They would appear to most people outside the United States, to be an immoral stance against basic human liberty and freedoms, one of which is to be able to walk down the street, without wondering whether or not your life is in danger.

Gun laws vary from state to state causing many outsiders to shake their heads in disbelief. The State of Arizona, with its slack gun laws, which includes the "Open Carry Rule", is a case in point. It states:

Arizona is an "open carry" state, which means that anyone can legally carry any (legal) weapon in the open, without any permits, as long as the weapon is:

- Kept in a holster or scabbard
- At least partially visible on your person, or;
- Kept in a container or the glove compartment of a vehicle (still must be holstered, however)[27]

This means that it is perfectly legal to carry a loaded handgun or revolver on a belt holster, out in the open, while you walk down the street, and no special permits are required.

Arizona also endorses "Concealed Carry Permits", also known as CCWs. These permits allow anyone to carry a weapon on their person out of sight. They are available to anyone who meets the state of Arizona's (rather lax) criteria:

- Be at least 21 years of age
- Have no felony convictions
- Be in the country legally
- Pass a Department of Public Safety approved firearm safety course (can be done in most community colleges)[28]

It is important to note that Arizona does not distinguish between resident and non-resident, or indeed even between US citizen and permanent resident. The only requirement is that you are NOT an illegal alien; any other person is eligible for a concealed carry permit.

The only conclusion that one can make is that if the United States wants to reduce gun-related deaths, they will need to change their culture, which has been a way of life for over 200 years. This will not happen overnight and may even take generations. First, there needs to be a will to change. This starts with massive re-education of the public by citing some of the examples above. Only in this way will the ethical majority recognise that change to the gun culture is not only desirable, but also essential, if they wish to protect their fellow man. Second, they may need to change their constitution and come up with a set of laws which bans certain automatic rifles and pistols, while at the same time making it much more difficult to obtain a licence for all firearms. Perhaps the lawmakers could take a lesson from the Australian model, as shown in fig. 1.2. The figures speak for themselves.

This is a huge task for any president to ask of Congress, given the influence of the National Rifle Association, particularly with the Republican Party. However, until the morally repugnant gun laws in the United States are changed, the deaths will continue to escalate, leaving a sad indictment on the American way of life, in the eyes of the rest of the civilised world.

Chapter 2

The Sanctity of Life

∞∞∞∞

The 4th July 1776, Independence Day in the United States is etched in every American's mind as one of the most significant events in American history. It was the day that the Declaration of Independence was adopted by the Second Continental Congress, the second section of which states:

> We hold these truths to be self-evident, that all men are created equal, that they are endowed by their Creator with certain unalienable Rights that among these are Life, Liberty and the pursuit of Happiness.[29]

To a large degree, this passage from the Declaration of Independence has become the justification of those who support the "sanctity of life" philosophy in the United States. One only needs to look at the role of the Catholic Church and the belief of most evangelical Christians, to get a clearer understanding on how most Americans currently think on this subject.

Abortion, the Death Penalty and Human Cloning

The sanctity of life has been a divisive issue for many years. It encompasses such areas as abortion, contraception, euthanasia, cloning, embryo research, genetic engineering and the death penalty. It also encroaches on the politically sensitive issues of war, torture and rendition, which we will cover in a later chapter. In order to get a clearer understanding of these on-going debates, we need to look more closely at what the proponents and opponents views are on each of these topics and the effects they have on the moral fabric of America.

There can be no debate about where the Catholic Church stands on this issue. Many articles have been published and countless sermons have been given on this very subject. Perhaps it can best be summed up by the following observation:

The sexual revolution of the 1960s brought challenging issues for the Church. Pope Paul VI's 1968 encyclical *Humanae Vitae* affirmed the sanctity of life from conception to natural death and rejected the use of contraception; both abortion and euthanasia were considered to be murder.[30]

This is further supported in an interview between Zenit, a non-profit newsagency supporting the principles of Catholicism and Father Victor Pajares, a bioethicist, who teaches at the School of Bioethics of the Regina Apostolorum Pontifical University. In this interview, Father Pajares debates the meaning of the term "quality of life" and how it relates to "sanctity of life". When asked the question, "Is there a wholesome ethic that can combine both elements; quality and sanctity of life?" This was his response;

> "We can identify it in the mainstream Catholic moral tradition, which is based on these three principles: defence of all human lives against intentional killing, mandatory use only of ordinary means to preserve health and life, and promotion of compassion and solidarity especially toward the most exposed in society.
>
> These three principles comprise both sanctity and quality of life. And so the Catholic ethic is not faltering in theory".[31]

While the position of the Catholic Church is unwavering, the same cannot be said of the politically powerful evangelical Protestants in the United States. While most may consider deliberate abortion as immoral, there are some denominations, such as the Evangelical Lutheran Church of America, which is more permissive of abortion.[32] Still other Christian denominations can be considered as pro-choice, when it comes to abortion. However, there are sizable minorities in all religious groups that disagree with their denomination's stance on abortion, such as the group, Catholics for Free Choice.[33]

So how does all this translate into how mainstream America thinks? The answer may be found in a Gallup poll conducted on 7th-10th May 2009. In this poll, Gallup found that 51% of Americans calling themselves "pro-life" on the issue of abortion and 42% "'pro-choice." This is the first time a majority of US adults have identified themselves as pro-life since Gallup began asking this question in 1995.[34] The article on the FaithWorld website also made an interesting observation. Some 70% of Republican Party supporters are likely to label themselves as pro-lifers. This compares with just 33% of pro-lifers who support the Democrats.

This should not come as any great surprise, as the article suggests:

> Much of the opposition to abortion in America has been faith-based, led mostly though not exclusively by conservative Catholics and evangelicals. The latter in particular have for decades been a key base of support for the Republican Party.[35]

Regardless of one's political leanings, there is ample evidence to suggest that the sanctity of life is paramount in the thinking of most evangelicals and Catholics. On the surface, this appears to be in sync with the ethics of their respective religious leaders. So, if the sanctity of life is held to be so sacred, then how is it that the majority within these same two religious groups still dogmatically favour the death penalty on one hand, while opposing abortion and euthanasia on the other. To many on the outside, this seems to be such a double standard that it borders on hypocrisy. Yet the statistics confirm this observation.

Overall, support for the death penalty has been steadily falling since the late 1980's when 80% of Americans favoured executing murderers. By 2010, this figure had fallen dramatically to just 64%. Nevertheless, according to one survey taken in mid-2010, 74% of white evangelicals and 68% of white Catholics support the death penalty.[36] The death penalty is morally abhorrent in the opinion of most western countries, where it is no longer practiced. This includes all western European nations and all other major English speaking nations such as, Canada, Great Britain, Australia and New Zealand. As we can observe in fig. 2.1, the United States is surrounded by nine other countries, most of which have dubious forms of legal systems.

Fig 2.1 (number of executions by country)

Rank	Country	Number Executed in 2010[37]	Form of Legal System[38]
1	People's Republic of China	5000	Civil Law
2	Iran	252	Islamic Law
3	North Korea	60	Unknown
4	Yemen	53	Islamic Law
5	United States	46	US Common Law
6	Saudi Arabia	27	Islamic Law
7	Libya	18	Islamic Law
8	Syria	17	Islamic Law
9	Bangladesh	9	English Common Law
10	Somalia	8	Unknown

If the United States professes to be the leader of the civilised world in terms of morality, then continuing with the death penalty, will do little to enhance its credibility. Not only is it contrary to the religious acceptance of the sanctity of life, it is often open to legal arguments as to whether innocent people are being executed. Since 1992, 15 people on death row have been exonerated as a result of DNA evidence.[39] One publication has listed 8 inmates that have been "executed, but possibly innocent".[40] Another article claims that at least 39 executions have been carried out in the United States, despite the evidence of innocence or serious doubt about guilt.[41]

But there is another serious discrepancy in the morality of the legal system and this is the role that one's race plays in capital convictions. In a recent study, which analysed all capital defendants in the State of Georgia, came up with the following statistics:

Fewer than 40% of Georgia homicide cases involve white victims, but in 87% of the cases in which a death sentence is imposed, the victim is white. White-victim cases are roughly eleven times more likely than black-victim cases to result in a sentence of death.

Further examination of the death penalty in the United States indicates that not only is there a bias against blacks and the poor, but there is also a bias depending where one lives. Since 1976, more than 1,200 people have been executed in the United States; 75% of them took place in southern states—and over 37% in Texas alone.[42] Yet another article further highlights these discrepancies:

According to data from DPIC, 15 US counties accounted for 30% of the executions since 1976 – which is less than

1% of counties in the country, and less than 1% of the total counties in all death penalty states. Nine of these counties are in Texas, and three are in Alabama.[43]

As well as the high-profile moral issues on abortion and the death penalty, people are also currently debating the legality of euthanasia. From a purely ethical perspective, the question really comes down to who has the legal right to determine when one dies? Is it the state, the church or the individual? There is no question that those of deep religious faith would more than likely disagree with the concept of euthanasia. While many might say that this is their prerogative, some secular people might take a different view. However, the statistics indicated through Gallup polling, tell a surprising story. According to a 2005 analysis, 75% of Americans support allowing a doctor to take the life of an individual, who is suffering from an incurable disease and wanting to die. Among evangelical Christians, 61% were in favour, while 75% of Catholics supported euthanasia. Does this indicate that there is a double standard when it comes to the sanctity of life amongst the devout in the United States? Perhaps that question is best left to the conscience of the individual.

On the subject of human cloning, the opinion polls are almost unanimous. They consistently indicate that between 84% and 90% of people in the United States are morally opposed to human cloning. However, 62% of the people support research into the use of stem cells obtained from human embryos.[44] These figures are not too far removed from other international surveys. In one such survey, which included samples from Indonesia, Kenya, Sweden and America, the negative view of religious respondents was 73.9%, compared to 73.8% of non-religious respondents.[45] Here at least, we can conclude that the ethics of the "sanctity of life" principle prevails almost universally.

Chapter 3

Climate Change

∞∞∞

There is a familiar saying that "Nero fiddled while Rome burned." Although this is most likely an urban legend, given that Nero played the lyre and was away from Rome at the time of the fire,[46] the expression is still used today, when someone (individual, media, politician or government) turns a blind eye to serious matters happening all around them. The acceptance and desire to tackle the very causes of climate change is very much on the back burner in the eyes of the average American.

This is supported by a Gallup poll in March 2012, which indicated that 42% of Americans believe that the media is overstating the problem of climate change, while only 31% say that the media is underestimating it.[47] Interestingly, 67% of Republicans and 20% of Democrats say that media coverage of climate change is exaggerated.

Perhaps the most disturbing aspect of this poll is that only 53% of the American public believe that climate change is due to human activities, while 41% believe it is due to natural cycles.[48] This is in direct conflict with the scientific community who are actively involved in climatology and related sciences. A survey by Kendall Zimmerman in 2008, which was given to over 3,000 climate scientists (90% from the US), asked just 9 questions on climate change. The most interesting result was on the question on whether they thought that human activity was a significant factor in rising global temperatures. Some 97% of climatologists who are active publishers on climate change agreed with the question.[49] So how can the American public get it so wrong?

There are probably two main reasons for this. First, people largely believe what they read in the newspapers, hear on the radio or see on the TV, when it comes to news. But increasingly, they believe what is being claimed in forums, blogs and social media. In an effort to be seen as being fair and balanced in the media, climate change sceptics get disproportionate coverage compared to the vast majority of scientists, who agree on the human contribution to climate change. This should be a cause for alarm.

An Oxford University study, which examined 3000 articles from the UK, USA, Brazil, India, China and France, found that 80% of the climate change sceptic articles were found in the UK and US press.[50] This huge imbalance gives the uniformed reader the impression that the scientific community is totally divided on the subject, and this is certainly not the case. This is reminiscent of the Y2K scare in late 1999, or that the world was coming to an end on 21 Dec 2012. The media at times can be totally irresponsible by continuing to write stories, which have absolutely no basis. Another example has to do with the authenticity of President Obama's birth certificate. Just because this was challenged by Donald Trump, it was deemed to be newsworthy. Unfortunately, this is how urban myths get started, particularly amongst the naïve and uneducated. In a recent Bloomberg report, it was claimed that 51% of Republican voters believe that Obama was not born in the US.[51] If people still believe this myth, then it's not surprising that climate change deniers are getting so much credence through the press.

It's time the press stopped hiding behind the coattails of corporations and politicians who have vested interests in promoting the anti-climate change rhetoric. But asking them to suddenly become ethical and to put the future of our planet ahead of their own financial outcomes, is perhaps expecting a little too much.

The second reason for the public scepticism is political. It started with the Kyoto Protocol on climate change, which was adopted on 11 Dec 1997 and ratified on 16 Feb 2005. By this date, 191 member states had signed and ratified the protocol. The only remaining signatory not to have ratified the protocol was the United States.[52] George Bush's intransigence on climate change undoubtedly led to Canada's withdrawal from the agreement in December 2011.[53] This was certainly the opinion of Paul Heinbecker, who helped negotiate Canada's position with regards to the protocol. Heinbecker stated;

"In my judgment the person who really torpedoed this whole enterprise was George Bush. Had the Americans participated ... by now there would be enormous pressure on the Chinese and the Indians to be accepting targets,"[54]

A further comment was made by John Bennett, executive director of the Sierra Club Canada who said;

> "Part of the plan rested on having new North American standards for cars and with George Bush in the White House that wasn't going to happen,"[55]

The question here is, why has the United States, isolated itself from the rest of the world on this extremely important issue? Is it a case of self-righteousness, arrogance, ignorance or the close association between the energy sector and the Bush administration? Or is it a combination of all these factors? To get some insight into these questions, we look at some extensive research papers that have been written on this very subject. In particular, we turn to an investigative report by Aaron McCright from Michigan State University and Riley Dunlap from Oklahoma State University, in a document entitled, *The Politicization of Climate Change and Polarization in the American Public's Views of Global Warming – 2001-2010.*[56]

In this report, McCright and Dunlap claim that the divide on climate science is politically motivated. Soon after Al Gore won the Nobel Peace Prize in 2007, for his efforts in alerting the world to the dangers of climate change, the Right side of politics including, conservative think tanks, media figures, Republicans in Congress and the Bush Administration, started an all-out assault on climate science and policy.

The conservative stance appears to be an ideological one. This side of politics champion individual freedoms, private property rights, limited government and the promotion of free markets.[57] It was the very threat that the United States would have to abide by an International agreement that caused the conservative Right to take a stance that was contrary to the overwhelming evidence that climate scientists had made available. The report infers that any treaty was seen as;

"a threat to sustained economic growth, the spread of free markets, the maintenance of national sovereignty and the continued abolition of government regulation – key goals of conservatives."[58] The report concludes that "conservatives and Republicans are more likely to dispute or deny the scientific consensus and the claims of the environmental community, thereby defending the industrial capitalist system."[59]

The real problem, it seems comes down to a particular demographic – Conservative White Males (CWMs) in the United States. McCright and Dunlap analysed 10 national public opinion polls and found out that:

- 14% of the general public doesn't worry about climate change at all, but among CWMs the percentage jumps to 39%.
- 32% of adults deny there is a scientific consensus on climate change, but 59% of CWMs deny what the overwhelming majority of the world's scientists have said.
- 3 adults in 10 don't believe recent global temperature increases are primarily caused by human activity. Twice that many – 6 CWMs out of every ten – feel that way.[60]

These are interesting statistics, posing the question – why is it so? It appears that there are a number of factors at work here. An article in Time Science in 2011 made the following observation:

Fossil-fuel companies like Exxon and Peabody Energy — which obviously have a business interest in slowing any attempt to reduce carbon emissions — have combined with traditionally conservative corporate groups like the US Chamber of Commerce and conservative foundations like the Koch brothers' *Americans for Prosperity*, to raise doubts about the basic validity of what is, essentially, a settled scientific truth. That message gets amplified by conservative think tanks — like the *Cato Institute* and the *American Enterprise Institute* — and then picked up by conservative media outlets on the Internet and cable TV.[61]

Yet this seems to be mainly an American phenomenon. It appears that Europe and most other developed countries accept the fact climate change is not only real, but is largely caused by humans and is already upon us. In the United States, there is a political divide between the liberal democrats, climate scientists and environmentalists on the left and climate deniers, CWMs and most Republican politicians on the right.

Some would say that this is how true democracy works and it shows that people are free to make up their own minds. Others believe that the tipping point, beyond which time climate change will be irreversible, is rapidly approaching. Meanwhile, the stance taken by American (and Canadian) conservatives continues to bring that inevitable date even closer. Will it be a case of; Conservatives fiddle while the world burns? Future historians will be the judge of that.

.

Chapter 4

Racism

∞∞∞∞∞

The 6th December 1865 was a momentous day in American history. It was the day that the Thirteenth Amendment to the United States Constitution, which effectively abolished slavery was adopted. In essence the amendment stated:

Section 1. Neither slavery nor involuntary servitude, except as a punishment for crime whereof the party shall have been duly convicted, shall exist within the United States, or any place subject to their jurisdiction.

Section 2. Congress shall have power to enforce this article by appropriate legislation.[62]

This was quickly followed by the Fourteenth Amendment, which guaranteed civil rights in the states, in 1868 and then by the Fifteenth Amendment in 1870, which banned racial voting restrictions. The text of the amendment is as follows:

Section 1. The right of citizens of the United States to vote shall not be denied or abridged by the United States or by any State on account of race, color, or previous condition of servitude.

Section 2. The Congress shall have power to enforce this article by appropriate legislation.[63]

While these three amendments were deemed to be a huge step in treating African-Americans as equal to white Americans, nothing could be further from the truth. Over 100 years later, Rev. Martin Luther King Jr., was killed while still fighting for civil rights for African-Americans, on 4th April 1968.[64] For 100 years, African-Americans have been treated as second class citizens. Their fate was all but assured by President Woodrow Wilson in 1913, who ordered the complete segregation of the federal Civil Service.[65] This meant that coloured people would be forced to go to separate schools and use separate public toilets, trains and buses. They were even required to sit on separate park benches and drink from different water fountains.[66]

Segregation was seen as being highly immoral by most other civilised societies and often likened to apartheid in South Africa. It was clear that both state and federal governments were unprepared to tackle this forced discrimination as it could potentially cause the loss of support to any political party which pursued it. If change were to occur, it would have to come from people in the streets, who demanded nothing more than being treated as equals.

Perhaps the real turning point came in Montgomery, Alabama, in December 1955, when Rosa Parks refused to give up her seat to a white passenger and move to the back of the bus, with the rest of the black passengers.[67] This single act of disobedience was the main cause of the Montgomery Bus Boycott[68] and her stance became the international icon against racial segregation. This event was all the more surprising given that President Harry S Truman ended segregation in the United States Armed Forces on 26th July 1948.[69]

Today, there are no longer any segregation laws requiring the separation of African-Americans from white Americans. But in many ways, racism is still rife within the United States. In the nearly 150 years since slavery was abolished, there was not enough government action or willingness by the white majority to rectify this moral injustice. Blacks were forced to move to the inner suburbs of large American cities in order to get employment in unskilled or semi-skilled labour. This concentration of the black community in small inner-city areas soon became the ghettos of America.[70] This, in itself, had a disastrous impact on the black people. One of the major contributors to their marginalisation was the practice of redlining.

Although the term redlining was coined in the late 1960s by sociologist John McKnight, the actual practice got its start with the National Housing Act of 1934, which established the Federal Housing Administration (FHA).[71] Through this agency, the federal government withheld mortgage capital to inner-city neighbourhoods, making it difficult, if not impossible for families in these areas to purchase homes.[72] In 1935, the Home Owners Loan Corporation looked at 239 cities and created "residential security maps, to indicate which areas were deemed ineligible to receive financing as determined by the Federal Home Loan Bank Board.[73]

But the discrimination that was brought about by redlining didn't just stop at receiving finance. The practice also denied or increased the cost of services to anyone living in these areas. These included; banking, insurance, access to jobs,[74] access to health care and in some cases even supermarkets.[75] These areas were based solely on the socio-demographic description of the area and not on an individual's ability to pay. Since blacks who could afford to pay were often not welcome in white communities, they were forced to live in redlined areas, where they were unable to secure a mortgage loan or have access to many other services as listed above. Another effect of redlining was the lowering property values in these areas, forcing landlords to abandon their properties, leaving them to serve as havens for drug dealing and other illegal activities.[76]

Needless to say, the problems of racism that exist today have their roots in the relative lack of foresight and inaction of all governments, since slavery was overturned. The legacy of this inaction has left many of the African-American population stranded in the ghettos, with lower education opportunities, lower access to health services and more likely to be attracted to a life of drugs and crime. This fact is reflected in the current incarceration figures as stated in an article on America's Wire:

One of every 15 African-American men is in a US prison or jail compared with one of every 36 Hispanic men and one of every 106 white men. Moreover, scores of African-American men are affected by chronic unemployment, lack of education, poverty and poor health outcomes.[77]

As if this situation is not bad enough, it appears that even the American justice system treats African-Americans differently to white Americans as indicated in Chapter 1.

Rodney King Case

Another example is the Rodney King case in 1991, where King was brutally bashed by at least four LA police officers, while other officers stood by and looked on, without interfering. A subsequent court case, heard in front of an all-white jury found the police officers not guilty, sparking the 1992 Los Angeles riots, which left 53 dead and 2,000 injured.[78] Fortunately, in this instance, common sense eventually prevailed, when a federal trial was held for civil rights violations and two of the police officers were found to be guilty and subsequently jailed.[79]

Quartavious Davis Case

Quartavious Davis is a 20 year old African American, who lived in a poor, predominantly black neighbourhood, south of Miami. He was receiving $674 a month from Social Services, as he had a learning disability and suffered from bipolar disorder.[80] Between October and December 2010, he and five accomplices robbed a number of commercial establishments. It was claimed by his accomplices at his trial that he carried a gun. Although no one was hurt during these robberies, the court found him guilty of the crimes and sentenced him to 162 years jail. His accomplices, who cut plea bargains, didn't have to stand trial and received jail terms from nine to twenty-two years.[81]

There is no question that Davis should be punished for his crimes. But given the fact that this was his first offence, the punishment does not fit the crime. There is no other way to describe this sentence, except as an indictment on the American judicial system. It makes a mockery out of claims by American politicians who complain about human rights abuses in other countries.

A consequence of these ridiculous sentences is that the United States, with 5% of the world's population has 25% of the world's prisoners – most of them black.[82] It would be extremely difficult to conceive of any possibility that a similar penalty would be handed out to a white person, who had committed the same offences. Cases such as these, confirms the view of many, that racism in the United States is still very much alive.

The fact that these circumstances still exist is an absolute disgrace and should be on the conscience of all ethically minded Americans. While it is easy to point the finger at past government policies, the fact that little has changed for African-Americans and other minorities, is the responsibility of everyone who had sat idly by and let these situations occur. Perhaps the privileged people on the right side of the red line might have taken a different view if they were forced to walk in their shoes, even for a short period of time. Sadly, even in the 21st century, many African-Americans are destined to remain marginalised and isolated in the political wilderness of indifference.

Part II

Lost Morality in Big Business

America's Lost Morality

Chapter 5

Wall $treet

∞∞∞∞

The United States has often been criticised for its immoral and sometimes inhumane actions, when it comes to its foreign policy. But immorality and the abuse of power is not strictly the domain of government or the military. Big business, it appears, is not immune from this criticism.

In this chapter, we examine how excesses in Wall Street, coupled with the lack of regulation, have led to the rapid deterioration of moral standards in many instances, which caused the global financial meltdown in 2007-2008.

In the movie *Wall Street* starring Michael Douglas, the mantra that has often been quoted since, is that "greed is good". It sounds simple enough. After all, it's the holy grail of western capitalism, where the most important thing that matters is continual high returns to the shareholders and exorbitant salaries to corporate executives. Unfortunately, this philosophy often involves huge risk taking, which is largely practised in a deregulated market. This inevitably creates a boom-bust cycle, such as we have recently witnessed. The resultant crash saw house prices drop by 33%,[83] unemployment rise to 9.9% in October 2009[84] and the US deficit skyrocket to more than $15 trillion.[85]

First, let's examine the prime causes of the Global Financial Crisis (GFC). When the housing bubble peaked and burst in 2007, it caused the value of financial securities to tumble rapidly. This in turn, led to the collapse of global markets and consumer confidence, resulting in the decline of economic activity, followed by a recession. In April 2011, the United States Senate issued the Levin-Coburn report[86], which analysed the reasons behind the economic collapse. It was a comprehensive bipartisan 635 page document that took over two years to compile. It stated in part;

"...that the crisis was not a natural disaster, but the result of high risk, complex financial products; undisclosed conflicts of interest; and the failure of regulators, the credit rating agencies, and the market itself to rein in the excesses of Wall Street."

It is also clear that much of the crisis was a direct result of US Government policy from the 1970's onward, which emphasised deregulation of the financial institutions. Another area of concern was the so-named "shadow banking system", comprising investment banks and hedge funds. In many ways, these institutions were as important as commercial banks to the US economy, but were subject to even less regulation. In a speech to the Economic Club of New York, Timothy Geithner, the then President and CEO of the Federal Reserve Bank of New York, stated;

"I do not believe it would be desirable or feasible to extend capital requirements to institutions such as hedge funds or private equity firms."[87]

It would be interesting to see whether he still maintains the same view today.

In January 2011, the US Financial Crisis Enquiry Commission was very certain about its conclusions;

"the crisis was avoidable and was caused by: Widespread failures in financial regulation, including the Federal Reserve's failure to stem the tide of toxic mortgages; Dramatic breakdowns in corporate governance including too many financial firms acting recklessly and taking on too much risk; An explosive mix of excessive borrowing and risk by households and Wall Street that put the financial system on a collision course with crisis; Key policy makers ill prepared for the crisis, lacking a full understanding of the financial system they oversaw; and systemic breaches in accountability and ethics at all levels."[88]

In spite of these findings, there does not appear to be any willingness on the part of government policymakers to further regulate the financial industry. They prefer to rely on the free market system of supply and demand, with little or no government control. Add a splash of self-regulation and there shouldn't be any problems.

Perhaps if the financial industry were to be held responsible for the millions of people who lost their homes or suffered financial losses as a result of stock market crashes and the world financial crisis, they might have taken fewer risks. Government regulation, while desirable to some degree, does not have to be the suffocating bogie that it is often made out to be. Australia is considered to have high regulation of the financial markets, by American standards. Yet, during the Global Financial Crisis, when US banks were begging for handouts from the government to rescue them from their own recklessness, the top four banks in Australia were rated amongst the top 20 safest in the world.[89] Not a bad result for a country of just 22 million people. Without government regulation, it is not surprising that no American banks ranked in the top 20.

Before leaving *Wall Street*, we need to make an observation about the "shadow banking" community of hedge funds and investment banks. During the financial crisis, these companies came under considerable scrutiny, mainly due to their practice of short selling shares to force prices down. It appeared to many that unscrupulous operators were making small fortunes at the expense of 'Mom and Dad" investors, who saw their savings dwindle at a time when they were losing their jobs and their homes. Financial institutions claim that short selling is necessary to provide the market with more accurate share prices, particularly with businesses which may be over-priced at the time. The problem may occur when an organisation talks down a company's performance, forcing its share value down, while simultaneously shorting the stock. While this form of market manipulation is illegal, it is easily disguised. The main tool that is used is commonly referred to as "short and distort"

(S&D). The following is an example as to how this might be achieved.

The first thing the S&D promoters need to do is to find a way to stimulate fear in a credible fashion. This is largely done by flooding on-line message boards with negative reports about a particular security, in such a way that optimistic information cannot be easily found. They will often use screen names to make the reader think that they are connected with the SEC or the Financial Industry Regulatory Authority (FINRA).[90]

If enough credible-looking information is generated, it isn't long before the investment community starts to panic and sells their shares before they drop any further. As the share price tumbles, stop losses are triggered, causing further deterioration in the stock's value. Meanwhile, the perpetrators of this crime are laughing all the way to the bank as they have shorted the stock, allowing them to buy it at a much lower price. While this type of S&D manoeuvre is more prominent in a bear market, it is still difficult for the regulators to trace and control.

It is necessary to point out that while these rogue operators are in the minority, they can inflict an inordinate amount of financial pain to the general public. Furthermore, in order for this strategy to work, it requires large volumes of shares to be traded, and these can only come from organisations with large holdings, such as hedge funds and investment banks. The "greed is good" philosophy may be good for the top 1% of income earners, but its ethical and moral value should be and must be seriously questioned.

Chapter 6

The Subprime Mortgage Crisis

∞∞∞∞

In order to begin to understand exactly what was behind the 2007 subprime mortgage crisis, we need to first take a closer look at the events that led up to it. We start with what is meant by the financial term "subprime lending". Simply put, it means making loans available to people who have little chance of acquiring a loan through traditional channels. These people may fall into a number of categories, including; people with no deposit, people with no credit history, people with a history of late payments or people with excessive debt.

Lending to these categories of borrowers was high risk, but as long as house prices kept rising, the private investment banks made an increasing number of these loans to the general public. However, there were two things they had not counted on; rising interest rates and falling house prices, as occurred in 2006-2007. This caused a rapid increase in foreclosures and defaults. So much so, that by Sept 2010, 23% of all US homes were worth less than the mortgage.[91] This high number of foreclosures, not only takes wealth away from the consumer, it also has a negative effect of the financial strength of banking institutions. So, who was to blame for this failure? Well, there were many factors, a few of which are highlighted in this chapter.

The Consumer

It is easy for the consumer to blame someone else for their misfortune. That is human nature. However, in this instance, the consumer must bear some of the responsibility. Borrowers could see the rapid increase in house prices, which rose some 127% between 1997 and 2006.[92] This massive increase resulted in two trends; those with existing mortgages taking out second mortgages to finance their consumer spending and those who could not get a loan through traditional banks, because of their low credit ratings, wanting to climb onto the bandwagon. Many of this latter group were talked into 2-28 loans, where they were offered a lower introductory fixed rate of interest for the first two years, followed by 28 years at a variable rate, known as adjustable rate mortgages or ARM. It was in the halcyon days, when household savings declined, but consumer spending and mortgages increased. In fact in 1974, household debt was only 60% of disposable personal income. By 2008, this figure had more than doubled to 134%.[93]

The same high risk borrowers knew that they would be struggling to covert to the higher interest rates after the two year period ended. But they were relying on high rates of appreciation in that time frame, which would allow them to refinance their mortgage. But as house prices started to decline, refinancing became more difficult. By September 2008, average

US house prices had actually fallen by 20% from just two years earlier.[94] This created a huge increase in mortgage defaults and foreclosures, to the point whereby Sept 2009, 14.4% of all US mortgages were either delinquent or in foreclosure.[95] Economist Robert Shiller summed up the housing bubble this way;

> "Speculative bubbles are fuelled by contagious optimism, seemingly impervious to facts, that often takes hold when prices are rising. Bubbles are primarily social phenomena; until we understand and address the psychology that fuels them, they're going to keep forming."[96]

Banking Industry's High Risk Practices

Mortgage plans

By 2005, the lenders were taking increasingly more risks to gain the business, regardless of the outcome. First, there was SIVA (stated income, verified assets loans). Under the SIVA plan, borrowers did not have to show proof of income. They just needed to show that they had money in the bank. This plan was quickly followed by NIVA (no income, verified assets). With these types of loans the lender did not even need proof of employment. But even this was not enough to satisfy the greed of the subprime lenders. They finally came up with NINA (no income, no assets). This meant that almost anyone could get a loan.[97] These policies, accompanied by interest only loans and perhaps even more damning was the option ARM. These were loans whereby the borrower could have the option of how much they paid each month. It meant that in many cases, their mortgage balances actually rose every month.[98]

But there was one final plan that was instrument in the unravelling of the subprime market. It was the use of automated loan approvals; loans that were made without the appropriate checks and balances.[99] By 2007, 40% of all subprime loans came from automatic loan approvals.[100]

Incentive bonuses

After the crash, many questions were being asked as to how subprime lenders could be so slack in their due diligence. It appears that the real reason was based on the Wall Street mantra of the time that "greed is good". Investment bankers had only one thing on their mind – the-end-of-year bonus. This observation can be summed up by a statement made by the New York State Comptroller's Office, which said;

> "In 2006, Wall Street executives took home bonuses totalling $23.9 billion. Wall Street traders were thinking of the bonus at the end of the year, not the long-term health of their firm. The whole system—from mortgage brokers to Wall Street risk managers—seemed tilted toward taking short-term risks while ignoring long-term obligations. The most damning evidence is that most of the people at the top of the banks didn't really understand how those [investments] worked." [101]

It is clear that incentive bonuses were based on the fees generated from financial products rather than how those products performed over time. Furthermore, executive compensation did not factor in the downside effects of increased risks taken by these executives.[102]

Mortgage Fraud

It was not enough for these mortgage lenders to provide high interest loans to dodgy borrowers and to take high bonuses based on the number of contracts they signed up. These highly unethical organisations went one step further, in a process called securitisation. This is where these mortgage brokers would pool all of their risky loans and sell them as bonds to unsuspecting investors.

Traditionally, this wasn't too risky a practice, especially when it was through Government Sponsored Enterprises (GSEs). First introduced in the 1980s, these bonds came with guarantees against default on the underlying mortgages.[103] The only risk was to the interest rate. But just prior to the subprime mortgage crisis, non-GSE banks, which weren't restricted by any government regulation, sold similar types of bonds, which not only didn't guarantee the interest rate, they also didn't guarantee the default risk.[104]

As a result of these high risk securitisation bonds, mortgage-backed securities nearly tripled between 1996 and 2007 to $7.3 trillion.[105] These in turn led to a dramatic increase in fraud cases against the mortgage originators and investment banks. The Financial Crisis Inquiry Commission reported in January 2011 that;

"...mortgage fraud...flourished in an environment of collapsing lending standards and lax regulation. The number of suspicious activity reports - reports of possible financial crimes filed by depository banks and their affiliates - related to mortgage fraud grew 20-fold between 1996 and 2005 and then more than doubled again between 2005 and 2009. One study places the losses resulting from fraud on mortgage loans made between 2005 and 2007 at $112 billion. Lenders made loans that they knew borrowers could not afford and that could cause massive losses to investors in mortgage securities."[106]

As at the end of 2011, the FBI reported 2,590 pending mortgage fraud investigations, with 71% involving losses of more than $1 million.[107]

Credit Ratings Agencies

Part of the problem in the subprime mortgage crisis was that many of the Mortgage-Backed Securities (MBSs) were given investment grade ratings by credit ratings agencies, despite the fact that these MBSs were based on risky subprime loans.[108] Many claim that these high ratings were as a result of the agencies being paid by investment banks, thereby creating a conflict of interest.[109] After a lengthy investigation, the SEC approved measures that would strengthen the oversight of credit ratings agencies. As a result, between Q3 2007 and Q2 2008, credit ratings agencies lowered the ratings on $1.9 trillion worth of MBSs. The flow-on effect was to considerably lower the stock price on many financial institutions.[110] The Financial Crisis Inquiry Commission reported in January 2011 that;

> "The three credit rating agencies were key enablers of the financial meltdown. The mortgage-related securities at the heart of the crisis could not have been marketed and sold without their seal of approval. Investors relied on them, often blindly. In some cases, they were obligated to use them, or regulatory capital standards were hinged on them. This crisis could not have happened without the rating agencies. Their ratings helped the market soar and their downgrades through 2007 and 2008 wreaked havoc across markets and firms."[111]

Government Policies

While there is no question that the combination of mortgage lender greed, customer ignorance and rating agency collaboration, were instrumental in the cause of the Global Financial Crisis, the US government policies had a significant role to play. The SEC put it most succinctly when it claimed that self-regulation of investment banks contributed to the crisis. But in many ways, the SEC is responsible for the lack of regulation, when it relaxed rules in 2004 that allowed investment banks to increase the level of debt causing the growth in MBSs and the support of subprime mortgages.[112]

It will come as no surprise to learn that the two sides of politics disagree as to whether the credit crisis was as a result of too much regulation or too little regulation. Conservatives suggest that over-regulation aimed at increasing home ownership for lower income families was the main cause.

Liberals on the other hand, pointed to the fact that GSE loans were far less risky than those securitised by lightly-regulated Wall Street banks.[113] More importantly, liberals suggested that companies that lobbied the government most aggressively were the same companies that had the riskiest lending practices. These same companies also lobbied for relief from regulations that were aimed at limiting their risk taking.[114]

One final piece of legislation that had an adverse effect on the financial sector was the Commodity Futures Modernization Act of 2000. This exempted derivatives from regulation, supervision, trading on established exchanges and capital reserve requirements.[115] Warren Buffet did not look favourably at derivatives, describing them as "financial weapons of mass destruction" in 2003.[116] Seeing the results of ongoing slack regulation in the financial markets, perhaps Buffet was right.

Chapter 7

Big Oil and Gas

∞∞∞

Oil reserves

Most people would agree that we are fast approaching a time when the world's oil demand will outstrip supply. The estimated known reserves of oil in December 2005 were only 1292.6 billion barrels,[117] while the estimated world usage in 2008 was just under 32 billion barrels per annum. As you can see by the chart in Appendix B, which originates from 2001, if no new oil reserves are found, the world can expect to run out of oil around 2037.

However, there are factors which could affect the outcome of these projections, as highlighted below:

1) Exponential growth in demand for cars in developing countries such as China and India may *increase* consumption

2) Alternative energy sources, such as biofuels, natural gas and electric cars may *reduce* oil consumption

But by far the most challenging threat to these projections is the figure indicated in the "world supply" column made by the Oil and Gas Journal in 2005.[118] These figures do not take into account the dramatic upward re-assessment of estimated reserves by OPEC during the 1980s. At this time, OPEC revised its rules, which set its production quotas partially based on each country's reserves. As a result, many countries suddenly found extra reserves as indicated in the table below. Another interesting observation is that although hundreds of billions of barrels have been extracted from the fields, reserve levels have not declined.

Fig 7.1 (Dubious increases in OPEC reserves of oil)

Declared reaserves with suspicious increases (in billion of barrels) *Colin Campbell. SunWorld 80-95*

Year	Abu Dhabi	Dubai	Iran	Iraq	Kuwait	Saudi Arabia	Venezuela
1980	28.00	1.40	58.00	31.00	65.40	163.35	17.87
1981	29.00	1.40	57.50	30.00	65.90	166.00	17.95
1982	20.60	1.27	57.00	29.70	64.48	164.60	20.30
1983	30.51	1.44	55.31	**41.00**	64.23	162.40	21.50
1984	30.40	1.44	51.00	43.00	63.90	166.00	24.85
1985	30.50	1.44	48.50	44.50	**90.00**	169.00	25.85
1986	31.00	1.40	47.88	44.11	89.77	168.80	25.59
1987	31.00	1.35	48.80	47.10	91.92	166.57	25.00
1988	**92.21**	**4.00**	**92.85**	**100.00**	91.92	166.98	**56.30**
1989	92.20	4.00	92.85	100.00	91.92	169.97	58.08
1990	92.20	4.00	93.00	100.00	95.00	**258.00**	59.00
1991	92.20	4.00	93.00	100.00	94.00	258.00	59.00
1992	92.20	4.00	93.00	100.00	94.00	258.00	62.70
2004	92.20	4.00	**132.00**	**115.00**	99.00	259.00	**78.00**

The net effect of this overestimation is summed up by Sir David King, the UK government's former chief scientist, who suggests that global oil reserves have been overestimated by a third, which could cause shortages and price spikes in the very near future.[119]

It is clear that these statistics have been known for many years, yet they have continued to be ignored or denied by those organisations with vested interests. These organisations, popularly referred to as Big Oil, claim that the looming oil crisis is overstated. For example ExxonMobil's CEO testified to Congress that the price of oil should be no higher than $60-$70 a barrel.[120] Even Citigroup has jumped on the anti-peak oil bandwagon by claiming that the recent surge in North American production has "buried" the peak oil hypothesis.[121] Much of this bravado stems from the newly discovered shale oil fields of North Dakota. But to put this in context, these fields will produce only around 500,000 barrels a day;[122] a small fraction of the 80-90 million barrels the world uses each day.

Naturally it is in the interest of Big Oil to debunk the peak oil science as pure myth. In that way, they are able to keep prices (and profits) high and survive for a little longer. After all, if people were told the truth about the world's oil reserves, alternatives might be found more readily and Big Oil would cease to exist – at least in its present form.

Some estimates suggest that recoverable shale oil reserves in the United States could exceed 1 trillion barrels, which would extend our global oil consumption for another 15 years or so. (This can be easily shown through extrapolation of the table in Appendix B.) But extracting shale oil may not be commercially viable, as the production of shale oil has been hindered because of technical difficulties and costs.[123] In March 2011, the United States Bureau of Land Management called into question proposals in the US for commercial operations, stating that;

"There are no economically viable ways yet known to extract and process oil shale for commercial purposes."[124]

It seems that the thought of peak oil hypothesis as being "buried" may be somewhat premature.

However there is one other energy sector that appears to be gaining some momentum and that is the production of natural gas. Unfortunately, the hydraulic fracturing technique (fracking) used to extract the gas has come into serious criticism from environmental groups.

Fracking

The process of fracking involves pumping highly pressurised fluids, gases and chemicals deep into the rocky sub-terrain. The majority of the fluid is water – about 90%. This may seem harmless enough, but the average well consumes about 19 million litres (5 million US gallons) in its lifetime.[125] Given that there are over 150,000 wells currently in the United states, this equates to 750 billion US gallons of fresh water being used or approximately 2,400 gallons for every man, woman and child in the United States; this at a time when at least 36 States are suffering from water shortages.[126]

But the exorbitant volume of water that is needed to extract the natural gas is not the most worrisome feature. By far the most serious aspect of fracking is its use of chemicals. These additives include biocides, surfactants, viscosity-modifiers, and emulsifiers.[127]

While some are low in toxicity such as those used in cosmetics, soaps, detergent, polish and paint,[128] many others are harmful to humans. These include: benzene, a known carcinogen; lead, which damages the nervous system and causes brain disorders; ethylene glycol, also known as antifreeze, which can cause death; boric acid, which can result in kidney damage or death; methanol which is highly toxic and 2-butoxyethanol, which can cause haemolysis.[129]

If these toxic chemicals weren't enough to sway the lawmakers against fracking, then what about the injection of radioactive tracers to determine the injection profile and the location of fractures? Admittedly, some of these tracers have a short half-life, but others, such as Cobalt-60 have a half-life of 5.27 years.[130]

In 2011, the US House of Representatives conducted a report investigating the use of chemicals in the hydraulic fracturing process. It found that out of 2,500 products used, more than 650 of these contained chemicals that were considered to be carcinogens under the Safe Drinking Water Act or listed as hazardous air pollutants.[131] There were also 279 products that had at least one component listed as being "proprietary" or "trade secret" and therefore were not subject to scrutiny by the US House of Representatives committee.[132]

Perhaps the most immoral aspect of fracking was how the Bush administration was quick to exempt oil and gas companies from environmental legislation. These include:

- Comprehensive Environmental Response, Compensation, and Liability Act
- Resource Conservation and Recovery Act
- Safe Drinking Water Act
- Clean Water Act
- Clean Air Act
- National Environmental Policy Act
- Toxic Release Inventory under the Emergency Planning and Community Right-to-Know Act[133]

The long term detrimental effects of fracking have yet to be fully realised. To date, there have been many cases of ground water pollution, air pollution through escaping methane, headaches, diarrhoea, nosebleeds, dizziness and many other health related problems.[134] While a cause and effect relationship has not yet been fully established, in 2012, researchers from the Colorado School of Public Health showed that air pollution caused by fracking may contribute to "acute and chronic health problems" for those living near drilling sites.[135]

Unfortunately, we see yet again that where there is a conflict between business and morality, business will win out almost every time, with the help of state and federal governments of all persuasions. One example of this is a University of Texas study which stated that "fracturing has no direct link to water pollution". But close scrutiny of this research project proves the lack of independence from organisations with vested interests. Statoil was involved with a $5m research grant with University of Texas' Bureau of Economic Geology in September 2011. Its program director,

Ian Duncan, was the senior contributor for the parts of the UT study to do with the environmental impacts of shale gas development.[136] As with many other aspects of American business, the moral ethics of fracking is almost non-existent. Sadly, there doesn't appear to be any change to this attitude in the foreseeable future, as long as the power gods of Big Oil and Government continue to ignore the health and environmental needs of the other 99% of Americans.

Chapter 8

Corporate Environmental Disasters

∞∞∞∞

L arge corporates have a sordid history of destroying the environment and not admitting any wrongdoing, until such a time that action is taken through the courts. Many corporate environmental disasters have made worldwide headlines and despite public protest, most are ignored by the uncaring corporate bosses. As we have seen with fracking, oil and gas companies head the large list of companies that have been responsible for environmental damage, many of which have affected the health of local residents. Some examples are listed below.

Pacific Gas and Electric

One of the most highly publicised cases that has come to the fore in people's minds is the case against Pacific Gas and Electric (PG&E). Through the sheer determination of a young legal clerk named Erin Brockovich, a case was constructed against the company for contaminating the local town water with hexavalent chromium, causing much illness for the 650 residents of the town of Hinkley, California. The chemical was used to combat erosion in the cooling tower and the waste water was discharged to unlined ponds at the site. Some of the waste water percolated into the groundwater, affecting an area about two miles long by one mile wide.[137] The case was finally settled in 1996 for $333 million, which was the largest settlement of its kind at the time.[138]

Brockovich and PG&E were involved with a similar case at Kettleman Hills Compressor Station in Kings County, California, some ten years later. Again, the suit was a result of chromium poisoning, which affected some 1,100 residents who had a wide range of illnesses. That suit settled for $295 million in 2006.[139] PG&E, although remorseful that the event had occurred, did not admit liability. PG&E spokesman Jon Tremayne said in a statement;

> "The differences between the plaintiffs and our company in the case, centred on opposing views of the health science on chromium. Although the settlement does not resolve these differences, we believe it is best to move forward."[140]

To add further insult to the people of Kettleman, the Environmental Working Group claimed in December 2005 that PG&E's alleged attempts to corrupt a previous medical study on chromium-6's carcinogenic effects.[141]

Although the PG&E case has been well-publicised, as a result of the movie *Erin Brockovich*, there have been several other major American corporates which have been found wanting with regard to the environment. I am certain that if every disaster was written about, they would fill several volumes. But for the purpose of *America's Lost Morality*, we will be mentioning only some of the larger ones, together with their settlement amounts.

Exxon Valdez

It was on 4th March 1989, when the oil carrier, Exxon Valdez, struck Bligh Reef in Alaska's Prince William Sound. As a result of the accident, the ship spilled some 42 million litres[142] (11 million US gallons) of crude along nearly 2,000 kilometres (1,300 miles) of shoreline and 28,000 square kilometres (11,000 square miles) of ocean.[143]

The original court case was heard by an Anchorage jury, which awarded $287 million for actual damage and $5 billion for punitive damages. Exxon appealed the punitive damages several times. It was reduced to $2.5 billion in the first instance, but after 19 years of litigation, the Supreme Court, in a 5-3 decision, ordered that the punitive damages be reduced to just $507 million.[144] This decision angered environmentalists and put serious questions about the political impartialness of the Supreme Court.

John Passacantando, executive editor of Greenpeace USA, summed it this way;

"For the court to require a company that recorded a 2007 profit of $40.6 billion and that posted the highest quarterly results in US corporate history in February to pay a mere $500 million in punitive damages to the affected Alaskans makes a mockery of justice,"

Union Carbide

Union Carbide India Limited (UCIL) owned and operated a pesticide plant in Bhopal, India. On the night of 2nd December, 1984, a leak of metho-isocyanate gas and other chemicals from the plant[145] resulted in the immediate deaths of nearly 4,000 people,[146] and a further 8,000 in the years that followed.[147] There were a further 558,125 injuries, out of which 3,900 were severely injured.[148] After several court hearings in both the United States and India, UCIL came to an out-of-court settlement to pay $470 million for damages of the Bhopal disaster.[149] In 1991, the Indian Supreme Court ordered UCC and its subsidiary to voluntarily construct a 500 bed hospital in Bhopal at a cost of $17 million, to which the company agreed.[150]

Asarco

American Smelting and Refining Company (Asarco) is a subsidiary of the mining conglomerate Grupo Mexico. Asarco, based in Tucson, Arizona, had been in business for 110 years, before filing for Chapter 11 bankruptcy protection in 2005. The company was accused of gross environmental misconduct at numerous sites, including illegally burning hazardous waste products instead of disposing them properly, across 19 states. According to the government, the actions of Asarco caused lead and other toxic metals to travel downstream, polluting water and soil.[151]

Four years later, on 31st August 2009, the United States bankruptcy Court approved a plan, whereby Asarco's parent company Grupo Mexico would be allowed to take the company out of bankruptcy, on the condition that it paid for all environmental damages made by the company. The settlement, which was the largest in American bankruptcy history, was for $1.79 billion. It was used to fund environmental clean-up and restoration.[152]

Chevron

A recent television advertisement from Chevron claims that Chevron's work proves that a clean, safe, healthy environment can go hand in hand with meeting the world's energy needs. The spin is good, but can it match the reality?

Between 1973 and 1992, Texaco (now Chevron) developed the Lago Agrio oilfield in Ecuador. Since Texaco left in 1998, some 30,000 residents have mounted a class action against Chevron, claiming that the company discharged 68 billion cubic metres (18 billion US gallons) of toxic waste, causing illness and damaging forests and rivers.[153]

On 15 Feb 2011, a court in Ecuador ordered Chevron to pay as much as $18 billion in compensatory and punitive damages for the alleged dumping of toxic waste products by Texaco.[154] Chevron has refused to pay for any damages and compensation claims made by the court, claiming that they (Texaco) had already remediated their share of environmental impacts in Ecuador.[155] Meanwhile, 30,000 Ecuadorean citizens are left with just a shallow victory from their local courts. One suspects the outcome may have been substantially different had the alleged atrocities occurred on American soil.

But the controversy surrounding Chevron's dubious environmental claims does not solely rest in Ecuador. In Nigeria, they appear to have gone to extraordinary lengths to shut down a number of protesters, who were taking action against what they saw as negative environmental and social impact. The protesters, numbering only about 100 at the time, wanted to shut down Chevron's operation and were seeking reparation and clean-up.

It was claimed by the protesters that:

Chevron Nigeria was believed to have hired Nigerian government security agents to forcibly remove the protesters and to have provided the agents with Chevron-leased helicopters to transport their troops to and from the barge. The security forces allegedly shot four protesters, killing two, and captured and tortured a fifth.[156]

Although a US court exonerated Chevron from any wrongdoing, the people of Nigeria involved with the claim would certainly see it differently. As the old adage says, where there is smoke, there is fire. Perhaps we'll never know the whole truth of this sordid affair.

Environmental accidents will continue to occur in the future. That unfortunately is the high cost of doing business in dangerous environments. The challenge for business is to be more amenable to taking responsibility for their actions. In each of the above-mentioned cases, the large corporate in question, denied responsibility and fought tooth and nail in the courts over many years, before they were rightfully ordered to pay compensation to the hapless victims of their operations. It just strengthens the argument that where there is a conflict between profit and what is morally acceptable, profit will win on almost every occasion.

Chapter 9

Big Pharmaceuticals
and
Corruption in the FDA

∞∞∞

A recent survey by the Consumer Reports National Research Center in the United States into Drug Industry influence and Federal Drug Authority (FDA) corruption came up with some surprising results:

- 96% agreed the government should have the power to require warning labels on drugs with known safety problems. As Consumer Reports explains, "Right now, the Food and Drug Administration must negotiate safety warning labels with a drug maker."

- 84% agree that drug companies have "too much influence over the government officials who regulate them." More than two-thirds of those surveyed are concerned that drug companies actually pay the FDA to review and approve their drugs. Is it possible that drug companies are effectively the customers of the FDA?[157]

- 92% agree that pharmaceutical companies should disclose the results of ALL clinical trials, not just the ones with positive results that they wish to publicize.

- 93% think that the FDA should have the power to demand follow-up safety studies from drug companies. According to ACMA, the FDA has no authority to require follow-up safety studies on drugs after they are introduced to the market. This is a serious oversight shortfall, given that many problems with drugs only appear after widespread use. (Patients are widely used as guinea pigs in any new drug launch.)[158]

- 60% agreed that doctors and scientists with a financial conflict of interest should not be allowed to serve on FDA advisory boards. Currently, doctors who earn hundreds of thousands of dollars each year in "consulting fees" from drug companies are not only allowed to vote on the recommendations for FDA approval of their drugs, there is not even any FDA requirement to disclose such conflicts of interest.[159]

- 91% said they had seen a drug advertisement on television or in print (a "victory" accomplished by the FDA legalizing such ads in 1998), and 26% said they asked their doctor for a brand-name medication after learning about it from an advertisement. Big Pharmaceuticals and the FDA claim that the purpose of advertising is to "educate" patients about medical treatments. However, this must be seriously questioned when nearly 50% of Americans are on prescription drugs of some sort.[160]

- 75% agreed that the allowing of drug advertising has resulted in the over-prescribing of pharmaceuticals. 59% said the government should restrict pharmaceutical advertising, and 26% said they "strongly agree" with such restrictions.

The above statistics are not surprising given the unscrupulous relationship between Big Pharmaceuticals and the FDA. In 2009, the annual number of deaths (37,485) caused by improper/overprescribing and poor to non-existent monitoring of the use of tranquilizers, painkillers and stimulant drugs by American physicians, exceeded both the number of deaths from motor vehicle accidents (36,284) and firearms (31,228).[161] It comes as no surprise to find out that the US, with 5% of the world's population, consumes about 86% of the abovementioned drugs, worldwide.[162] When prescription drugs of all types are taken into consideration, the number of deaths is considerably higher. In a little known fact, more people die from prescription drugs each year than from illicit drugs. (Refer to fig 9.1 below).

Fig. 9.1 (Deaths from prescription and illicit drugs in the US)

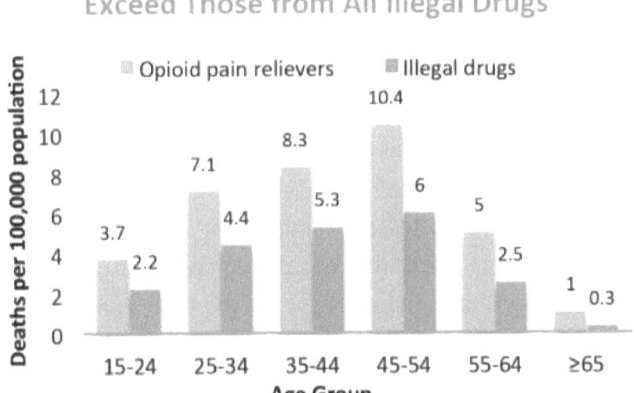

Source: CDC, Morbidity and Mortality Weekly Report, 60(43): 1489, 2011.

According to one United Nations report, 16 million Americans abuse over-the-counter medicine.[163] That's 6.4% of the population or nearly one person in 15. This trend is not surprising when the drug industry revenue statistics are analysed. In 2011, worldwide revenues from drug companies were estimated to be $880 billion. The United States, with 5% of the world population accounted for 37.5% of total drug revenue, or $330 billion.[164] Why is it that the American public are so addicted to prescription drugs? The answer comes down to ethics – or lack of them by Big Pharmaceuticals.

First, the pharmaceutical industry spent $855 million, more than any other industry, on lobbying activities from 1998 to 2006, according to the non-partisan Center for Public Integrity.[165] Second, the pharmaceutical industry advertising spend in 2011 was $2.5 billion according to Forbes.[166] Third, the widespread practice of payments to medical professionals has resulted in some doctors receiving in excess of $100,000 for speaking and consulting engagements. Under new laws, which force drug companies to disclose their payments to doctors and the health care profession, 12 US pharmaceuticals have paid 761.3 million in disclosed payments.[167]

There can be no question that continuing R & D by the pharmaceutical industry is as important as it is desirable. The problem occurs when the negatives outweigh the perceived benefits. How many people have to die or become addicted to prescription drugs, before some sense of morality becomes a priority amongst pharmaceutical industry executives? Common sense would indicate that these deplorable practices should not be allowed to continue in any form. Prescription drugs are essential in today's society, but the public should not be subjected to commercial advertising or indiscriminate issuing of prescriptions by unscrupulous health professionals. Finally, why is it necessary for the drug industry to have so many government lobbyists? (1,274 registered lobbyists according to USA Today)[168] Perhaps the government is just as complicit as the pharmaceuticals for the nation's sad, but real prescription drug addiction problem.

GlaxoSmithKline

In July 2012, GlaxoSmithKline (GSK) was fined $3 billion for marketing drugs for unauthorised use, holding back safety data and cheating the government's Medicaid program.[169] The company admitted that it promoted antidepressants Paxil and Wellbutrin for uses not approved by US authorities. In particular, it was promoting the use of these drugs to children and adolescents.[170] This was despite the fact that short term studies indicated that these antidepressants may increase suicidal thinking and behaviour in children under the age of 18.

Furthermore, GSK was accused of sponsoring a number of programs to promote off-label use of Paxil and Wellbutrin. According to US attorney, Carmen Ortiz;

"The sales force bribed physicians to prescribe GSK products using every imaginable form of high-priced entertainment, from Hawaiian vacations [and] paying doctors millions of dollars to go on speaking tours, to tickets to Madonna concerts."

The company also admitted that it held back data and made unsupported safety claims about Avandia, a drug used to treat diabetes. The settlement included $300 million in underpaid rebates to Medicaid.[171]

Although no criminal charges had been laid at the time of writing, the case highlights the lengths that corporations will go to in order to improve the bottom line. It proves yet again why the term "business ethics" can easily be perceived as an oxymoron.

The FDA Whistle blowers

In January 2009, an anonymous letter from an FDA insider was sent to John Pedesta on President Obama's transition team, describing widespread systemic corruption within the FDA.[172] The letter was written by a group of scientists on FDA letterhead, with their names blacked out for fear of retribution. A year later in March 2010, the FDA admitted that the letter was authentic and had been sent by someone within the FDA.

The letter mentions in particular, three specific events, which the authors felt needed to be investigated. These were;

The letter cites three dark chapters in FDA history:

- Former chief Andrew von Eschenbach's interference with the approval of a knee device.
- The approval of a breast cancer detection device by director of the Office of Device Evaluation Donna-Bea Tillman even though all FDA experts voted against it, following a phone call from Connecticut congressman Christopher Shays.
- And the approval by Daniel Schultz of a medical device that prevents tissue scarring against the unanimous opinion of his scientific staff.[173]

In another section of the letter, the authors wrote;

"... many other FDA managers who have failed to protect the American public, who have violated laws, rules, and regulations, who have suppressed or altered scientific or technological findings and conclusions, who have abused their power and authority, and who have engaged in illegal retaliation against those who speak out, have not been held accountable and remain in place."[174]

A legal opinion on the FDA

Another independent opinion on how the FDA abuses its position of authority and how public health may be at risk as a result, comes from Constitutional lawyer, Jonathan Emord. In a radio interview on Coast to Coast AM in 2010, Emord, who has defeated the FDA several times in federal court, makes some very interesting claims. A few of his comments on this radio program are stated below;

"The FDA doesn't conduct any scientific, clinical trial of any drug it approves. It relies entirely on the industry to determine whether the drug is safe or not."

"The tragedy is we really do have a system that is financially controlled by the drug industry, the influence is extraordinary, the evidence in support of that is immense...It's horrendous that an agency of the government that is commissioned purportedly for the purpose of protecting public health is more an agent of the drug industry."

In his book *The Rise of Tyranny*, Jonathan Emord claims that the FDA's Associate Director of the Office of Drug Safety, Dr David Graham, has been extremely critical of his own agency for its continual approval of drugs which are unsafe. Graham stated;

"The FDA is inherently biased in favour of the pharmaceutical industry. It views industry as its client whose interests it must represent and advance. It views its primary mission as approving as many drugs as it can, regardless of whether the drugs are safe or needed."[175]

Emord also states;

"We can perceive abuses whenever agency actions sacrifice fundamental rights to life, liberty, and property to yield outcomes favorable to a preferred regulatee. At FDA, the agency's Commissioner has repeatedly approved drugs that the agency's own medical reviewers have deemed too unsafe to enter the market, thus favoring the pharmaceutical company proponent of the drug over the American public.

The results have been catastrophic, leading to tens of thousands of deaths and injuries. Likewise, FDA maintains a pervasive censorship over therapeutic claims for foods and dietary supplements to ensure that the drug industry enjoys a federally enforced monopoly on the right to communicate treatment information.[176]

Jonathan Emord's greatest concern about the FDA is that they operate as a dictatorship and is unaccountable to the courts, the Congress or the American people.[177] If this is the case, as Emord claims, then the FDA and other federal agencies, which have the power to enact legislation with impunity, have much to answer for. Many people have died because they thought that their prescription drug was safe. How much further evidence is required before the whole system is re-evaluated? The time for action is now.

Chapter 10

Big Tobacco

∞∞∞

The man's name was Wayne McLaren, but not many knew him by his real name. He was a typical American man, living life with great expectations, until at the age of 49 he was diagnosed with lung cancer. Despite extensive chemotherapy, radiation therapy and the surgical removal of his left lung, the cancer spread to his brain and his life was tragically cut short at the age of 51. This is all too common a story, in every society, in every country. But Wayne McLaren had no way of knowing that an event that occurred in 1955, when he was only 14 years old, would change his life forever. In that year, a cigarette company that was struggling because of languishing sales, decided to change their image and appeal to a wider audience. They hired a ranch hand named Darrell Winfield, who, dressed in a cowboy outfit and always seen smoking a cigarette, became known as the *Marlboro Man.*[178]

The ad was accompanied with the line, "delivers the goods on flavour," and sales went far beyond expectations.[179] By the end of 1955, Marlboro sales returned some $5 billion in revenue; a staggering increase of 3,241% over the previous year.[180]

Over the next few decades, a number of other men played the role of the Marlboro Man, one of whom was Wayne McLaren. Two other Marlboro Men, David McLean and Dick Hammer also died of lung cancer.[181] However, Wayne McLaren recognised the error of his ways and became an active anti-smoking campaigner before he died in 1992.

Sadly, these personal tragedies did not deter the Big Tobacco companies from marketing their products in any other fashion other than to produce increased revenues. In one Wall Street Journal report, a tobacco company donated $125 thousand worth of food to a charity and then spent $21 million telling people about it.[182] While this had not broken any laws from a legal perspective, it is clearly unethical. The main purpose of the exercise was not the donation itself, but how the publicity behind the donation could best be converted into cigarette sales.

This should come as no surprise. Even today, the tobacco industry spends $12.4 billion each year on advertisements and promotions in the United States alone.[183] Considering that there are still 47 million smokers in the United States,[184] that's the equivalent of $0.72 per smoker every single day. So why does Big Tobacco spend so much every day? The answer is simple; because it's so effective. This is because on a worldwide basis, between 80,000 and 100,000 children start smoking each day.[185] Some 34% of these do so as a result of promotional activities by Big Tobacco companies.[186]

Philip Morris, the world's largest cigarette company spends more than $3 billion a year on advertising and promotion.[187]

Huge investments such as this by Big Tobacco, is obviously proving to be successful, as 15 billion cigarettes are sold around the world each day.[188]

In the past few years, American communities have become increasingly aware of the detrimental health aspects that smoking causes. In their bid to educate the public of the perils of smoking, in 2009 they spent some $700 million on tobacco control. But in the same year, Big Tobacco spent $12 billion on marketing and advertising.[189] As a result, the war against smoking seems to have stalled. Despite the numbers of people smoking having declined for three decades, the number has not changed over the past five years.[190] The exception is the State of California.

California has some of the toughest anti-smoking campaigns over the past 20 years. The results are outstanding. Smoking has dropped 40% and lung cancer rates are dropping four times faster than the national average.[191] While it's easy to point the finger at increased advertising by Big Tobacco, there is another rather disconcerting factor at work. Simply put, many of the State Governments are not taking the anti-smoking campaign seriously.

In an ABC News Video made in 2005, reporter Brian Ross made the following observations:

- As a result of a settlement with the tobacco industry in 1998, some $250 billion was to be given to the States over 25 years, with a view that much of this money would go to anti-smoking education
- In Virginia, $500,000 was used to improve a speedway

- Tobacco funds were used to upgrade a sprinkler system on a New York golf course
- Tobacco funds were used to build a new tobacco warehouse in North Carolina
- In Kentucky, funds were used to subsidise cattle farmers
- Overall, less than 3% of the 1998 settlement fund has gone to anti-smoking campaigns
- Last year, Kentucky received $109 million and spent only $50 thousand on anti-smoking education and advertising
- In Buffalo, New York, most went to paying off a budget deficit and waterfront projects. Not one penny was spent on anti-smoking
- In the last five years, Florida cut its spending from $70 million to just $1 million today
- Last year, States gave more to tobacco farmers than to tobacco control[192]

Despite the enormous success that California had achieved in previous years, even that State has taken a backward step. In 2012, tobacco generated revenue exceeded $70 billion. Yet California invested only $70 million on tobacco awareness campaigns, far short of the $441.9 million recommended by the CDC.[193]

When California was investing more on the program, it had a 50-1 return on investment in the form of health care savings, according to Richard Barnes, a researcher at the University of California's Center for Tobacco Research and Education.[194] At the time, CDC Director, Tom Frieden, estimated that 5 million lives could be saved over the next five years if all the States followed California's actions.[195]

With these sorts of projections, we have to seriously question the ethics of most State governments when it comes to tobacco awareness. It seems that millions more people will die prematurely, because of lack of interest or concern for the health and well-being of its citizens. How much longer will it take for this message to be understood? To paraphrase a Bob Dylan song, "The answer, my friends, is blowing in the *smoke-filled* (author's words added) wind."

Chapter 11

Dying for Fast Food

∞∞∞

Most of us live busy lives. Not only are we are working longer hours, but there has been a steady increase in two-income families and single parent families over the past few decades. Discretionary time is becoming scarcer and the days when most Moms stayed home to cook the family meals are long gone. As a result of this changing demographic, two industries have developed exponentially over the past 50 years; child care and fast food. While the jury may still be out on the long term effects of outsourced parenting on the children, there is absolutely no doubt about the harmful effects that the fast food industry has had on our health and on our environment.

The low cost and relative ease of fast food can be more of a necessity, than just a convenience for many families. In fact, there are so many choices in this market that it makes it easy for the occasional dinner out to become a way of life for these same families. The consequences of their fast food habit might be great for business, but it can be extremely costly in terms of health for the consumer.

Fast Food and the Link to Obesity

Obesity rates in the United States have been steadily climbing over the last fifteen years. In 2010, the CDC estimated that 35.7% of American adults are considered to be obese;[196] up from 19.4% in 1997.[197] Furthermore, children have not escaped this trend. Between 1980 and 2008, the percentage of obesity in children aged 6-11 went from 6.5% to 19.6%. In the same timeframe, obesity in teenagers more than tripled from 5% to 17.6%.[198] Apart from the detrimental health effects of obesity to the individual, there are also economic health costs to the community. John Cawley and Chad Meyerhoefer of Lehigh University calculated that obesity cost the United States $190 billion a year, which is 20.6% of the entire US healthcare expenditure.[199]

There are many reasons why people get obese; genetics, metabolism, behaviour, environment, culture and socio-economic status, but basically it all comes down to eating too many calories and not doing enough physical activity.[200] Given the fact that the rapid rise in obesity mirrors the rapid rise in fast food outlets, the question that needs to be asked is; what role has the fast food industry played in this phenomenon?

According to Dr David Ludwig, director of the obesity program at Children's Hospital Boston, nearly a third of US children eat fast food every day.[201] But Dr King is not surprised at the results, given that billions of dollars spent every year by fast food advertising, directed mainly at kids. Their unhealthy diet of fats, sugars and carbohydrates increased their intake by 187 calories per day, resulting in an average weight gain of six pounds per year.[202]

According to Business Insider, the total number of fast food restaurants in the United States is a staggering 221,000; that's one fast food restaurant for every 1,400 people.[203] Another research paper compared the number of fast food restaurants per capita in the 26 most developed economies and found a direct correlation between the number of restaurants and obesity. For example, Japan, has only .19 fast food outlets per 100,000 and has an obesity rate of only 3% - or about one-tenth that of America.[204]

Many believe that the current obesity epidemic and attraction to junk food comes down to unethical marketing practices by the fast food industry. There have been numerous research papers and books written on the subject, which support this assumption. Perhaps one of the most critical research papers on fast food marketing was published by FACTS (Food Advertising to Children and Teens Score), a health research team from Yale University.[205] The report is fairly extensive and well-researched and recommended reading for any parent with children or teens, who may have a leaning towards fast food. Listed below are just some of the highlights from their research:

- The fast food industry spent more than $4.2 billion in 2009 on TV advertising and other media advertising.
- Since 2003, advertising to pre-schoolers has increased by 21%; children by 34% and teens by 39%.
- McDonald's web-based marketing starts with children as young as 2 at Ronald.com.

- McDonald's 13 websites attracted 365,000 unique child visitors and 294,000 teen visitors each month in 2009.
- 84% of parents reported taking their children to a fast food restaurant at least once in the past week. 66% reported going to McDonald's.
- 40% of parents reported that their child asks to go to McDonald's at least once a week; 15% of pre-schoolers ask to go once a day.
- Teens between 13 and 18 ordered many of the highest-calorie, nutrient-poor items on the menu, averaging between 800-1500 calories, which is up to 5 times more than recommended by the American Dietetic Association for active teens.[206]
- Just 12 of the 3,069 possible kid's meal combinations met nutritional criteria for pre-schoolers; 15 met the criteria for older children.

There can be no question that parents must shoulder some of the responsibility of child obesity. But after several decades of fast food advertising, many of these same parents themselves are victims of past marketing campaigns.

Certainly, most fast food restaurants are trying to overcome growing media negativity by promoting healthy alternatives. But these are not the alternatives that are being promoted to children and teens. Instead, kids are continually drawn to the menu items, which are high in fat, sugar and salt, all of which will almost guarantee two results; obesity and a shorter lifespan. It's time that the fast food industry started thinking more about the well-being of their customers than the financial well-being of their executives and shareholders.

Fast Food Industry and the Environment

For many years, the fast food industry was indirectly complicit in the over-clearing of native rainforests in Brazil. Originally, it was Brazilian beef that was being used to feed the growing demand for hamburger meat in the United States and around the world. This was followed by a Greenpeace alert about Brazilian soy, which was used to feed beef and chicken, destined for fast food restaurants.[207]

Fortunately, through the efforts of Greenpeace and books like *Fast Food Nation* by Eric Schlosser,[208] the giants of the fast food industry have been forced to change their policies, which in the past, had contributed to large tracts of deforestation in Brazil. In a classic example of "strange bedfellows" McDonalds and Greenpeace teamed up to enforce a moratorium on the production of soy from newly deforested land.[209] Most would agree that this is a positive move. But there are still many other environmental issues, which need to be addressed.

One such area of concern has to do with corn. In a Scientific American article from 2008, it was suggested that the vast majority of fast food hamburger from McDonald's, Burger King and Wendy's comes from corn-fed cows.[210] But it just isn't hamburgers which rely on corn. There was also evidence of a corn diet in chicken sandwiches and even French fries, from being fried in corn oil.

While a diet of meat from corn-fed animals poses no known health effects, there are considerable environmental issues that need to be addressed, such as; drained water supplies, degraded soils and reliance on fossil fuels for fertilizers, pesticides and farm machinery fuel.[211] One side-effect is that humans may lose out on getting omega-3 fatty acids, which are vital for the development of nervous system tissue and heart health.[212]

Another area of increasing environmental concern, with regard to the fast food industry is in the area of packaging. When we consider that annual sales of the 400 largest fast food chains are nearly $300 billion,[213] then we can imagine the massive amount of packaging that this creates. Not only does the disposal of these products create a huge environmental waste disposal headache, but the actual manufacturing of these products are destroying the Southern Forests in the United States.[214] With nearly 100 paper mills in the area, fast food giants such as McDonald's, KFC, Pizza Hut, Wendy's and Taco Bell are major consumers of paper packaging sourced from this area.[215] Lauren Bennett, the Alliance Media Outreach Co-ordinator states;

"Every year millions of pounds of food packaging waste litter our roadways, clog our landfills and spoil our quality of life. Southern forests, the jewel of the American landscape, are being destroyed to bring you fried chicken, burgers and fries, and super-sized convenience in a glut of wrappers, boxes and cups."

However, experience tells us that we can't rely on the fast food industry if we really want effective changes that will benefit the well-being of our health, our forests and our planet. Change must start with the individual. In the end, we alone are responsible for our own individual health and how we use packaging. There are many green organisations, which are beginning to promote alternatives, which may help alleviate the growing concern. It is up to us to seek these groups out and to collectively take the massive action needed to make a difference.

Chapter 12

Sins of Monsanto

∞∞∞∞

Genetic modification

The first thing that comes to mind when the term "genetic modification" is used, is the company that is behind it - Monsanto. Whether the consumption of GM foods are detrimental to one's health is not the primary subject of this book. What must be questioned are the business strategies that Monsanto uses to ensure that their organisation is financially successful. Many of these strategies have little or no ethical value, which most people would see as being contrary to the American way of life.

To show just how belligerent and self-righteous Monsanto executives can be, let's review two statements made in the 1990s;

"If you put a label on genetically engineered food you might as well put a skull and crossbones on it."[216]

"Monsanto should not have to vouchsafe the safety of biotech food. Our interest is in selling as much of it as possible. Assuring its safety is the FDA's job."[217]

It is clear from these two statements alone that they have no regard for the health and welfare of the end consumer of their products. But just how far are they prepared to go?

The State of California looks like being the first state to insist on mandatory labelling laws, which will identify foods that have been genetically modified. A recent survey indicated that over 80% of Californians are in support of the labelling.[218] Similar discussions are taking place in Vermont, but the government is slow in passing labelling laws that the majority of people want. The reason – Monsanto has threatened to sue the State of Vermont if the legislation is passed. It's a classic example of corporate intimidation running roughshod over public interest. As at May 2012, the legislation has stalled, despite the fact that four separate polls found that more than 90% of Vermonters support requiring labels on food made with genetically modified seeds, reflecting the national trend.[219]

Should the California labelling laws get up, they will join 40 countries which have already enacted mandatory GM labelling, including all of Europe, Japan and China.[220]

Genetically modified crop contamination

Perhaps even more disturbing is how GM crop seeds are being spread by the wind to contaminate nearby organic farms. This can be disastrous to the farmer, who may be unable to sell his crops as they are no longer considered to be organic. But what makes these cases more worrisome is that the ethically bankrupt Monsanto executives will sue the organic farmer for illegally using their GM seed, which the wind has carried from nearby GM farms.

A well-publicised case in point is that of Canadian farmer Percy Schmeiser, who owned a 1400 acre canola farm in Saskatchewan. He had been working the farm successfully for 40 years, developing his own varieties and using his own seed. But when Monsanto accused him of patent infringement and demanded restitution for its seeds, he decided to fight back.

First, here is a little background. Most farmers were using Roundup to kill off all the weeds before planting the new season's crop of canola from seeds that they had gathered the previous year. Then Monsanto came up with genetically modified canola, *Roundup Ready*, which was completely immune to Roundup. While this sounds like it may be beneficial, there was a huge financial catch. Farmers using the new genetically modified canola had to purchase all future seeds from Monsanto each year. Many farmers, like Schmeiser chose not to go down that route.

The legal case was first heard in a Federal Court in Saskatoon, Saskatchewan from 5th-20th June 2000.[221] The Federal Court issued its findings on 29th March 2001, where Justice Andrew McKay upheld the validity of Monsanto's patented gene which it inserts into canola varieties to make them resistant to their herbicide Roundup.

However, Schmeiser appealed to the Supreme Court and in May 2004, it was determined that while Monsanto's patent was valid, Schmeiser did not have to pay any compensation to Monsanto.[222]

Another example was from North Dakota, where Monsanto sued Roger, Rodney and Greg Nelson for patent infringement, despite an independent body's ruling that it found no evidence of wrongdoing.[223] According to the North Dakota State Seed Arbitration Board;

"The evidence does not show, by the greater weight of the evidence, that Nelson Farm is infringing on any Monsanto patents for RR soybeans by planting, growing, and harvesting unlicensed saved RR soybean seed without authorization from Monsanto, or that Nelson Farm will continue to so infringe. Nelson Farm did not plant any saved RR soybean seed in 1998, 1999, or 2000."

The same article from CropChoice News claims that Monsanto was suing hundreds of farmers on the grounds of patent infringement. Once again, we see that where there is a conflict between profit and ethics, the dollar wins nearly every time.

Dioxin poisoning

Monsanto may well be wondering why they are considered to be one of the most despised organisations in the United States. Perhaps another example from Nitro, West Virginia may help explain the public perception.

In 1949, Monsanto had a chemical plant in Nitro, which was used in part, to manufacture the now banned chemical 2-4-5-T, which contained one of the most lethal chemicals known – dioxin. Dioxin has a half-life of 100 years when leached into the soil or embedded water systems. 2-4-5-T was used in the manufacturing of the infamous Agent Orange, which was used extensively during the Vietnam War. Today, the Veteran's Administration pays out regularly to veterans, who have suffered dioxin related cancer, birth defects in children, leukaemia, liver disease, heart disease, Parkinson's disease, heart disease and chloracne.[224] But the same cannot be said of Monsanto. Both Monsanto and Dow Chemical enjoy complete government immunity, as a result of a ruling by Judge Jack Weistein.[225]

Yet, despite an explosion in the Nitro plant in 1949, Monsanto had not paid out a single cent to the victims of Nitro suffering from dioxin injuries. Finally, after 7 years of litigation and a class action against Monsanto, the company has agreed to compensate the residents with a $93 million settlement.[226]

Agent Orange

During the Vietnam War, the United States sprayed 80 million litres (approximately 20 million US gallons) of chemical herbicides and defoliants between 1961 and 1971.[227] As previously mentioned, 2-4-5-T used to produce Agent Orange was extremely toxic. As a result, Vietnam claims that 400,000 people were killed or maimed and 500,000 children were born with birth defects.[228] Despite all the evidence of the destructive nature of Agent Orange, Monsanto executives still have the audacity to make outrageous claims. In 2004, Jill Montgomery, a spokesperson for Monsanto, said Monsanto should not be liable at all for injuries or deaths caused by Agent Orange, saying;

"We are sympathetic with people who believe they have been injured and understand their concern to find the cause, but reliable scientific evidence indicates that Agent Orange is not the cause of serious long-term health effects."[229]

It must be noted that as far as the Vietnam War is concerned the US government is just as liable for death, injury and suffering as the Agent Orange manufacturers. However, Monsanto and Dow Chemical must be jointly and severally held accountable for the use of Agent Orange for non-military purposes throughout the world.

Many countries have been adversely affected by the use of this chemical defoliant over the decades. These include: Canada, Australia, New Zealand, Malaya, Thailand, Korea and parts of the United States.[230] All would be justified in taking legal action against Monsanto and Dow Chemical and it will be interesting to see how this plays out.

But the ultimate insult to the people of Vietnam is the plan by Monsanto to sell GMO crops to the Vietnamese farmers.[231] Why, one might ask? So that they can sue all the organic farmers in Vietnam as they have done in the United States? Do these executives not have a conscience?

rBGH

BGH is a peptide hormone produced by the cow's pituitary gland.[232] Since 1994, it has been possible to synthesise the hormone using recombinant DNA technology. This practice is commonly known as recombinant bovine growth hormone or rBGH. This artificial growth hormone was first developed by Monsanto and marketed as Posilac, a brand now owned by Elanco Animal Health. However, as far back as 1995, medical research has confirmed that use of rBGH may speed the growth of human breast cancer and prostate cancer.[233] At that stage the Cancer Prevention Coalition recommended that the FDA withdraw its approval for rBGH. As a result, the use of rBGH as a supplement has been banned in 27 countries, including Canada, United Kingdom, Australia, New Zealand, Japan and the European Union. Interestingly, the FDA does not agree with all the other developed nations and approved the use of rBGH in the United States. It can be argued that the FDA is just as complicit in this issue as Monsanto. But the questionable role of the FDA, as discussed in a previous chapter, should be of little surprise.

So just how far will Monsanto go to protect its perceived right regarding this product? One example comes from Oakhurst Dairy in Maine, a dairy that has been owned and operated by the same family since 1921. In a response to consumer demand for milk that is free of rBGH, Oakhurst, along with many other dairies in the US, decided to inform their customers that milk from their dairy was hormone free. Monsanto sued Oakhurst claiming that they should not have the right to mention that their product did not contain rBGH.[234] Oakhurst settled out of court, but the message was loud and clear to all other dairy producers.

Over the past few years, many organisations are ignoring the claim by Monsanto and the FDA that rBGH poses no risks to human health and are labelling their products as artificial growth hormone free. Some simply refuse to buy dairy products from dairies which use rBGH. There is a growing list of companies that are choosing to accept the scientific verdict of all other developed nations over the claims of the FDA. These include; Safeway in the North West United States,[235] Starbucks[236] and Kroger.[237] Hopefully, it is only a matter of time before the educated and morally conscious consumer can convince their government leaders to ban these products once and for all.

PCBs

The only North American company that produced PCBs was Monsanto, under the trade name of Aroclor, between 1930 and 1977. PCBs or polychlorinated biphenyl were mainly used as dielectric and coolant fluids in transformers, capacitors and electric motors. They were also used as stabilising additives in flexible PVC coatings of electrical wiring and electronic components, pesticide extenders, cutting oils, reactive flame retardants, lubricating oils, hydraulic fluids, and many other chemical products.[238]

Although PCBs seemed to have a bright future, it soon became clear that the product was fraught with danger. The toxicity of these products had been known from the outset, but the findings which were done by the manufacturing companies themselves, were quickly dismissed as negligible. The most common adverse effect on humans was a skin condition known as chloracne. In Japan in 1968, 280kg of rice bran oil, contaminated with PCBs was used as chicken feed, resulting in the deaths of 400,000 chickens and mass poisoning of 14,000 people.[239]

Other studies have shown PCBs to be associated with specific types of cancer, such as cancer of the liver and breast cancer.[240] Although the production of PCBs was banned by the United States Congress in 1979, there were still serious questions raised as to Monsanto's knowledge of the dangers and its attempt to ignore or cover-up the potential hazards and threats to humans and to the environment.

In an article in the Washing Post on 1st January 2002, Michael Grunwald writes about the tragic events that occurred in a small Alabama town called Anniston. The townspeople lived, worked and played in one of the most polluted places in America, without knowledge of the contamination that was willingly caused by Monsanto. For 40 years they lived in ignorance of their toxic environment.[241]

During that time, Monsanto routinely discharged toxic waste into a west Anniston creek and dumped millions of pounds of PCBs into open-pit landfills.[242] Many company documents, which contained warnings, such as "Confidential" or "Read and Destroy", suggest that Monsanto executives were well aware of the detrimental effects of their actions. In 1966, Monsanto managers discovered that fish submerged into the west Anniston creek turned belly-up within 10 seconds, spurting blood and shedding skin.[243] In 1979, they discovered fish in another creek with 7,500 times the legal PCB limit.[244]

So how long had Monsanto known about the potential dangers of PCBs? Shortly after they purchased a 70 acre plant near Coldwater Mountain in 1935, a memo was distributed by management stating that PCBs "cannot be considered non-toxic (sic)". After a 1937 Harvard study suggesting that prolonged exposure to PCBs could cause liver damage, Monsanto began warning their customers that their workers should shower after every shift and be provided with clean work clothes every day.[245]

In 1997, Monsanto spun off its chemical division into a new company called Solutia Inc. But as far as the citizens of Anniston, Alabama are concerned, this did little to rectify the problem. According to Michael Grunwald from the Washington Post;

"Solutia has opposed proposals for comprehensive health studies as unnecessary. And it has not apologised for any of its contamination or deception."

It appears that the roots of unethical practices within Monsanto are extremely well-entrenched.

Chapter 13

Non-GM based Agriculture

∞∞∞∞

Agriculture is a vital industry in the United States, and is a net exporter of food. At the last census in 2007, there were 2.2 million farms, covering nearly 4 million square kilometres (over 912 million acres). In round numbers, the United States produces about $100 billion worth of livestock and a similar amount in crops every year.[246] But the agriculture industry is far from squeaky clean and faces many ethical issues across a wide range. These include: soil degradation, pesticides, environmental threats and child labour. As we have already discussed the trend towards growing GM crops in the previous chapter, we will only be focussing here on all other forms of agriculture.

Pesticides

Pesticide is a generic term for insecticides, herbicides, fungicides and other forms of substances used to control pests.

Although the use of pesticides is widespread, the United States Environmental Protection Agency has strict guidelines as to how they should be used. The EPA website states:

> The Endangered Species Act is intended to protect and promote the recovery of animals and plants that are in danger of becoming extinct due to the activities of people. Under the Act, EPA must ensure that use of pesticides it registers will not result in harm to the species listed by the US Fish and Wildlife Service as endangered and threatened, or harm to any habitat critical to the survival of those species.[247]

This seems to be fairly straightforward enough, but has it been effective? Below is a brief summary of some of the environmental and health issues as a direct result of pesticide use.

- According to the US Geological Survey, pesticides have polluted every stream and over 90% of wells sampled.[248]
- The National Academy of Sciences estimates that between 4,000 and 20,000 cases of cancer are caused per year by pesticide residues in food in allowable amounts.[249]
- The United States Department of Agriculture and the United States Fish and Wildlife Service estimate that between 6 and 14 million fish are killed by pesticides each year in the US.[250]

- The USDA and USFWS estimate that over 67 million birds are killed by pesticides each year in the US. [251]

The Pesticide Data Program, started by the USDA has tested over 60 different types of food for over 400 types of pesticides. The results from 2005 were quite disturbing. It found that in foods such as apples, lettuce and pears the percentage of pesticide residue found from their sample size of over 700 in each category, ranged between 87% and 98%.[252]

Also, according to the Pesticide Action Network North America (PANNA), testing by the CDC found that 93% of Americans tested by the CDC had traces of TCP, a metabolite of chlorpyrifos, which is a neurotoxic insecticide, in their urine. Banned from home use because of its risks to children, chlorpyrifos is part of a family of pesticides (organophosphates) linked to ADHD.[253]

The study also found that 99% of Americans tested positive for DDE, a breakdown product of DDT, even though DDT hasn't been used in the United States, since 1972. Women, who were exposed to DDT as girls, are 5 times more likely to develop breast cancer.[254]

Given the overwhelming evidence of the damaging effects of pesticide use, serious questions must be asked as to how this has been allowed to happen and what steps will be taken to rectify the situation? There can be no question that organic farming is less productive for the farmer and more costly for the consumer. But surely the time has come to place people's health and the state of the environment above the profits of large pesticide manufacturing companies.

Child labour

In the twenty-first century, it is hard to accept that child labour is still a growing worldwide problem. We have seen it in the textile, clothing and footwear industries, particularly emanating out of sweatshops in Asia. However repugnant these practices may be, the world accepts them by default, simply by purchasing goods that have been made from these places.

But many people might be surprised that these same practices are being used today in the United States agriculture industry. Each year, hundreds of thousands of children, some as young as 12, are hired by the industry in the United States. They are used to hoe cotton, pick fruit and vegetables, cut off onion roots, and to drive tractors.[255] These same workers often work for 10 hours or more a day, five to seven days a week. Some even start working part-time at the age of 6 or 7.[256] Often, they get paid less than minimum wage and are forced to buy their own tools, gloves and drinking water, which should be provided by law.[257]

As well, according to the Centre for Disease Control's National Institute for Occupational Safety and Health (NIOSH), children working in agriculture risk pesticide poisoning, serious injury and heart risk. They suffer fatalities at more than four times the rate of children working at other jobs and many employers did not even supply drinking water, hand washing facilities or toilets.[258]

One tragic result of this child abuse is that agricultural children drop out of school at four times the national rate. Yet, despite all of these facts, the United States government refuses to take the actions necessary to eliminate these heinous practices. According to Zama Coursen-Neff, deputy director of the children's rights division of Human Rights Watch;

"The US spends over $25 million a year – more than all other countries combined - to eliminate child labour abroad, yet is tolerating exploitive child labour in its own back yard."[259]

Coursen-Neff also makes the point that child labour on US farms violates international legal obligations under the International Labor Organisation (ILO).[260] In 2010, 12 children under the age of 16 died as a result of work-related injuries in the US agriculture industry.[261] How many more kids have to die unnecessarily before farmers and regulators decide that child labour is totally unacceptable in developed countries in the 21st century? Hopefully, common sense will prevail sooner rather than later.

Factory Farming

The acronym that is currently used to describe the controversial method of intense animal farming is AFO (animal feeding operation) or CAFO (concentrated animal feeding operation). By using just a small area of land, these operations congregate animals, feed, manure and urine, dead animals, and production operations.[262] The difference between the two methods is the number of animals that are involved. Both methods feature highly concentrated confinement areas with no pasture or grazing land.[263] An example of how CAFOs have changed the farming environment in the United States can be seen in figures relating to pig farms. In1966, it took 1 million farms to house 57 million pigs. Today the same numbers of pigs are farmed in less than 80,000 farms.[264]

On the surface, there appears to be sound economic reasons for this trend including:

- Lower monetary cost – has a tendency to produce food that can be sold at a lower cost to the consumer
- Standardisation – allows for increased consistency and control over product output, compared to traditional farming methods
- Development of new technologies – the advent of CAFOs has allowed for new technologies to emerge, which reduce production cost and increase business profits with less resources consumption

While these benefits are certainly valuable assets to the animal farmer and to the end consumer, there is a downside to CAFO operations.

Human health

The dangers to human health to people who work on CAFO operations are considerable, according to the CDC. Workers can develop lung disease and may catch infections that transmit from animals to humans, such as tuberculosis.[265] Another source of concern is the use of pesticides, which can accumulate in animals raised on factory farms. These same pesticides can eventually end up in humans, causing health problems.[266]

Also, the CDC claims that chemical, bacterial and viral compounds from animal waste can travel into the soil and water, causing possible health effects to nearby residents.[267] The CDC also identified a number of pollutants that come directly from the discharge of animal waste. They claim that the use of antibiotics may create antibiotic resistant pathogens, such as parasites, bacteria and viruses. As well, ammonia, nitrogen and phosphorous can contaminate drinking water.[268] A report by Science Daily indicated that 47% of all meat and poultry sold in US supermarkets was contaminated with S. aureus and that 52% of those bacteria were resistant to at least three classes of antibiotics.[269] One of the senior authors of the report, said;

"The fact that drug-resistant S. aureus was so prevalent, and likely came from the food animals themselves, is troubling, and demands attention to how antibiotics are used in food-animal production today."[270]

While CAFOs may save the farmer and possibly the consumer some money, no amount of saving can be justified if human health is put at risk.

Animal health and welfare

One example of animal cruelty is how 60%-70% of the six million breeding sows in the United States are confined during pregnancy and indeed, most of their adult life, in cages which are only .61m x 2.1m in size (7ft x 2ft).[271] These cages are referred to as gestation crates. This practice is extremely contentious as even pork producers admit that sows will fight if housed in pens. Animal welfare advocates regard them as one of the most inhumane features of intensive animal production.[272] In Europe, these crates have been banned, effective from 2013, after the 4th week of pregnancy. The largest pork producer in the US said in 2007 that it will be phasing out gestation crates by 2017.[273] Unfortunately, this meant another 10 years of suffering for the sows.

A report in 2007 maintained that overcrowding and confinement has a detrimental effect of the animal's health. Lack of exercise weakens their bones and muscles. Intensive poultry farms are a breeding ground for viral mutation and transmission. With the advent of globalisation and the transfer of goods to international destinations, the potential for the spread of disease is high.[274] Furthermore, these practices can lead to contamination of the meat from viruses and bacteria. This is easy to understand when feedlot animals often spend time standing in their own waste.[275] A single dairy farm with just 2,500 cows can produce as much waste as a city of 411,000 people, making the transmission of viruses highly likely. To make things worse, animals often have residual manure on their bodies when they go to slaughter.

Another area of contention is the cage size used in the poultry industry. In the United States, the current recommended standard is $430cm^2 - 550cm^2$ ($67in^2 - 86in^2$).[276] This is about the size of an A4 (letter) sheet of paper per hen. If these cramped living conditions weren't bad enough, the birds must be debeaked; a procedure which causes acute pain, according to many scientists.[277]

There is only one conclusion that can be made. To confine poultry to these cages is totally inhumane and a disgrace on the industry and government legislators who allow it to happen. One can only imagine the outrage that would occur if the family pets were to be confined in a similar manner.

Environmental and financial impact

New research has found that CAFOs are having a severe and detrimental effect on the environment. One such study made the following observations:

- Significant amounts of toxic animal waste are released into water and air without environmental controls in place, causing pollution to air, soil, and the water supply.
- This pollution, in turn, appears to be a causative factor in the increased illness rates observed among people who live near CAFO facilities.
- The widespread, routine administration of antibiotics to confined hogs increases bacterial drug resistance and thereby endangers public health.
- Land values and quality of life in areas near CAFOs have been shown to decrease markedly and consistently.
- The local economy suffers rather than improves, and small-scale farming declines.[278]

It is claimed that factory farms generate 500 million tons of waste product every year.[279] But unlike cities, which are required to treat their sewerage before discharging it to the environment, factory farmers are under no such obligation. CAPOs typically store their liquid waste in cesspits known as "lagoons", while the solid waste products are retained in piles called "litter". This may sound safe enough, but after heavy rainfalls, waste runoff gets into the waterways, resulting in massive fish kills and dangerous contamination of water with bacteria.[280]

There have been numerous papers, articles and books on this subject and what we have highlighted is just a sample of the environmental effects of this type factory farming.

Use of Antibiotics

As stated in the chapter on fast foods, corn is fed to cows as part of the fattening process. Although not harmful to humans, it is detrimental to the animals, as their stomachs are designed to breakdown cellulose in grass. This has led to an exponential rise in the use of antibiotics in these very same animals. So much so that one Scientific American report claimed that some 25 million pounds (11 million kg) of antibiotics were used each year to feed cows, chickens and pigs.[281] This represents about 70% of all antibiotics made in the United States.

Unfortunately, the high use of antibiotics has been increasingly shown to have potentially devastating effects on human health. A 2003 World Health Organisation (WHO) made the following statement;

"There is clear evidence of the human health consequences (from agricultural use of antibiotics, including) infections that would not have otherwise occurred, increased frequency of treatment failures (in some cases death) and increased severity of infections."[282]

A study in 2005, estimated that antibiotic-resistant infections would add about $50 billion a year to the annual cost of American healthcare.[283] The case against the high use of antibiotics in animal feed has been around since 1977. Fortunately, in March 2012, US Magistrates Judge, Theodore Katz has ordered the FDA to withdraw support of antibiotic use in animal feed, unless the drug makers can prove that such uses are safe.[284] In his judgement, Katz stated;

"In the intervening years, (since 1977) the scientific evidence of the risks to human health from the widespread use of antibiotics in livestock has grown, and there is no evidence that the FDA has changed its position that such uses are not shown to be safe,"

It is clear that the agriculture industry has much to answer for. But it may still be a long battle, before farmers and the FDA come to some agreement that will be beneficial to the American population in the long term. Interestingly, the European Union banned the routine use of antibiotics in meat in 2006.[285] In conclusion, the independent Pew Commission reported that;

"...the factory farm system often poses unacceptable risks to public health, the environment and the welfare of the animals, and recommended that significant changes be implemented immediately."[286]

Chapter 14

People vs Profit

∞∞∞

The main goal for any business is to make a profit for its shareholders. Most people would not have too many issues with this as being acceptable business practice. After all, if there was no profit, the business would soon find itself in debt and eventually may be forced to close its doors permanently to the detriment of its workers and their families.

In difficult times, such as when the country is in a recession, many companies have little choice but to reduce staff numbers, in order to survive. The problem occurs when a company is making good profits, but still wields the axe onto many of its domestic staff. There are many reasons for this, but the two that stand out, are outsourcing and the use of overseas sweatshops.

Outsourcing

According to an article in the Wall Street Journal, major multinational companies in the United States have cut their domestic employee numbers by 2.9 million in the first decade of the 21st century, while during the same time outsourcing some 2.4 million jobs.[287] These companies include the likes of General Electric, Caterpillar, Microsoft, Wal-Mart, Chevron, Cisco, Intel, Stanley Works, Merck, United Technologies, and Oracle.[288] Another way to express this trend is through the following graph:

Fig. 14.1 (Domestic job losses vs outsourcing)

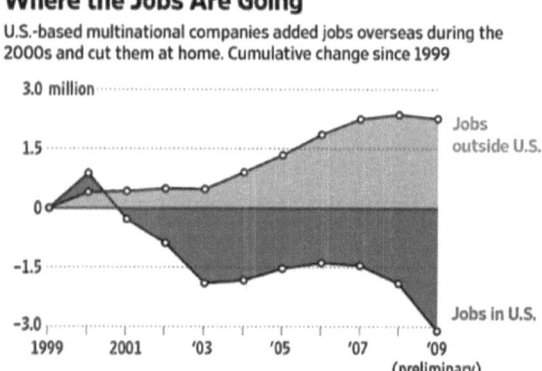

Where the Jobs Are Going

U.S.-based multinational companies added jobs overseas during the 2000s and cut them at home. Cumulative change since 1999

A 2003 report by the McKinsey Global Institute made the claim that outsourcing delivers large and sustainable measurements to the United States economy.[289] The same McKinsey report also claimed that for every dollar spent outsourcing, it creates between $1.12 and $1.14 of additional economic activity in the United States. Through outsourcing, companies can reduce IT and other service costs by up to 60%., thereby making them more competitive in a global market.[290]

No doubt that these seem to be impressive figures, but if they can be taken seriously, why are large US multinationals trying to hide the extent of their outsourcing? Companies such as Pfizer, Hewlett Packard, Apple and AT&T have not disclosed the breakdown between domestic and overseas jobs to the SEC since 2000.[291] To add insult to injury, two of these companies, Pfizer and Apple have joined a growing number of companies that are lobbying for tax breaks on the money they have made overseas, claiming that any money brought back into the US would spur hiring.[292] One wonders what the nearly 3 million people who lost their jobs to outsourcing would think of that idea. It is becoming increasingly clear that company economists can always put a favourable spin on their decision-making policies. The spin, however, is designed to satisfy the shareholders. The employees, it seems, are but disposable pawns in a global game of chess, designed to make the 1% of money earners even wealthier and more powerful.

Sweatshops

A sweatshop is largely regarded as a workplace which has substandard working conditions for its employees. Typically, they are underpaid, work long hours and often in appalling conditions. Many use child labour and some are forced to work in hazardous conditions. Over the past couple of decades, the public has become increasingly aware of the atrocious conditions that are synonymous with many US business practices. Many companies, particularly in the textile, clothing and footwear markets have closed down their American factories, in order to source cheaper labour costs overseas.

The arguments given by these multinationals is that by cutting manufacturing costs, they can sell the end-product to the American consumer at a vastly reduced price, so everyone benefits. But critics disagree. They claim that large multinationals are knowingly choosing to whitewash the abuses in order to save their bottom line. One example that is given refers to a Honduras sweatshop, where a worker is paid $0.24 for making a $50 Sean John sweatshirt.[293] Meanwhile Sean John Clothing Inc. had revenues exceeding $450 million in 2004.[294]

Perhaps one of the most notorious organisations that has its success rooted in the sweatshops of Southeast Asia is Nike. The company first started using sweatshops for their footwear in the 1970s, mainly in South Korea and Taiwan. Then, as their economies developed and labour became more expensive, Nike pulled the plug on these two countries and took their business to cheaper sweatshops in Indonesia, China and Vietnam.[295] When workers in these countries started to make demands for better wages and working conditions, Nike factories closed and moved to yet a different location, which operated at lower costs. This strategy has served Nike well. In the year ending 31st May 2011, they made a gross profit of $9.87 billion.[296] It's difficult to know for sure just how many outsourced workers Nike employ, but if they had one million workers in their sweatshops, they could afford to give each of them a bonus of $1,000, while only reducing their profit to $8.87 billion. This would have an enormous impact on the sweatshop workers' quality of life. But this will not happen, simply because workers are there for the sole purpose of lining the pockets of senior executives and the company shareholders.

According to *The Economist*, a sewing machine operator in Bangladesh is entitled by law to a minimum monthly salary of $18.53; in Honduras, a worker in an export industry earns $139 a month and in China's Guangdong province, the minimum wage is $63.75 a month, although this is supposedly subsidised with board and lodging.[297]

Just to give a further example of how sweatshops have changed the landscape in the United States, Levi Strauss, unable to afford the $12 an hour in American wages, closed its last plant in 2004. Twenty years earlier, Levi's had more than 60 factories in the United States.

It is fair to say that many clothing and footwear industries have taken note of the massive public outrage over the use of sweatshops and are now monitoring their factories much more closely. The challenge for the industry is that much of the monitoring is done by company employees and therefore may not be seen as being objective or independent.

Apple and Foxconn – A Case in Point

It seems that the old adage, "the bigger they are, the harder they fall" might apply in the case of Apple Inc. Apple have been receiving a spate of negative press about the working conditions in their overseas manufacturing plants, namely Foxconn. Foxconn, a Taiwanese company has manufacturing plants in Asia, Europe and Latin America, including 13 factories in China, in 9 cities. Its main business is the manufacturing of well-known technology products such as iPhone, Kindle, PlayStation, Wii and Xbox 360. Its factories are huge by western standards; the largest being in Longhua, Shenzhen, where hundreds of thousands of workers (some estimate up to 450,000)[298] are employed at the Longhua Science & Technology Park, a walled campus.[299] Another Foxconn city is located at Zhengzhou Technology Park, where some 120,000 employees work.[300] At the heart of the controversy regarding sweatshops is the appalling working conditions as exemplified at some of Foxconn's factories.

Foxconn's working conditions

Workers in the two biggest Foxconn Technology Parks in China complain about their extremely harsh working conditions; certainly oppressive by Western standards. Many work excessive overtime, sometimes seven days a week. Under-age workers are often employed and hazardous waste is improperly disposed, causing serious problems with employees' health.[301] In 2010, employees at an Apple supplier's plant in Eastern China were ordered to use poisonous chemicals to clean iPhone screens, causing injury to 137 workers.[302] In 2011, 7 people were killed and 77 injured at two separate explosions at iPad factories. According to a Chinese report, Apple had been alerted to the hazardous conditions inside the plant.

Nicholas Ashford, a former chairman of the National Advisory Committee on Occupational Safety and Health, stated;

"If Apple was warned, and didn't act, that's reprehensible, but what's morally repugnant in one country is accepted business practices in another, and companies take advantage of that."

This may be so, but one Foxconn ex-employee, Li Mingqi sees things a little differently. He said;

"Apple never cared about anything other than increasing product quality and decreasing production cost."[303]

Li helped managed the Chengdu factory where one of the explosions occurred.

Life for most employees was extremely difficult. Apart from the long hours of work and overtime, workers lived in cramped quarters, with up to 20 people crammed into a 3 bedroom apartment.[304] Their average monthly salaries ranged from $US358 to $US455.[305] According to a report by the auditors from the Fair Labor Association (FLA), more than 60% said their wages fall short of their basic needs. The FLA was hired by Apple to audit overseas suppliers.[306]

The investigation by the FLA also found that all three factories exceeded Chinese legal limits of 60 hours per week. Furthermore, 14% of Foxconn's workers may not receive the compensation they are owed. In the same report, more than 43% of workers surveyed claimed that they had experienced or witnessed some form of work-related accident.[307] The work conditions were so severe that in 2010, 10 young workers committed suicide and 3 others had tried.[308]

Apple's response to these claims

Since 2005, Apple has had a code of conduct for its suppliers. In part, it states that;

"It requires suppliers to provide safe and healthy working conditions, to use fair hiring practices, to treat their workers with dignity and respect, and to adhere to environmentally responsible practices in manufacturing. To that end, the code includes standards in the areas of Labor and Human Rights, Health and Safety, Environmental Impact, and Ethics and Management Commitment."[309]

Apple's CEO, Tim Cook's response was in the form of a company-wide e-mail. In it he wrote;

"We care about every worker in our worldwide supply chain. Any accident is deeply troubling, and any issue with working conditions is cause for concern. Any suggestion that we don't care is patently false and offensive to us."[310]

In light of the recent bad publicity against Apple's main component supplier, Foxconn, Apple have recently announced 25% pay increases for their Chinese workers. (The figures quoted previously include these pay rises.) Cook has also pledged to "raise the bar of manufacturing companies everywhere."[311]

There can be no question that Apple has been trying to improve working conditions at Foxconn, in order to overcome adverse publicity. While this is a step in the right direction, much more needs to be done. The difficulty is that people reading the FLA reports seem to be aghast at the wages and conditions on offer. What we need to understand is that for many of these Chinese employees, conditions at Foxconn are much better than most other options available to them.

The real question that remains is this. Given the current economic downturn and high unemployment in the United States, would it not be more ethical to produce their products locally, thereby stimulating the US economy? Certainly, this would add a fair bit to the cost of an iPad or iPhone, but this cost could be easily absorbed by consumers, and more products would be sold if there were more consumers working. The other unknown quantity is whether or not Apple would ever have acted, if the facts about workers' conditions weren't made public.

In the 2nd quarter 2012, Apple revenue increased to $39.2 billion and its gross profit was $11.6 billion. Extended for the full year, it would show a profit of $46 billion. Surely, it would be easy for a qualified accountant to calculate what the effect on gross profits and prices would be if the manufacturing was all done locally in the United States. But that is not the way business works today. The only consideration in today's business environment is profit before people. Surely, there must be a better way.

Income Inequality and Wealth Distribution

The vast discrepancy in incomes and wealth in the United States was the founding cornerstone of the Occupy Wall Street movement, which held its first rally on 17 Sept 2011, in the Wall Street precinct of New York City. The OWS movement is trying to address the growing disparity between the top 1% of income earners and the rest of the population. Looking at the graph below, they have reason for their concern.[312]

Fig.14.2 (Average income growth rates for the top 1% and all others)

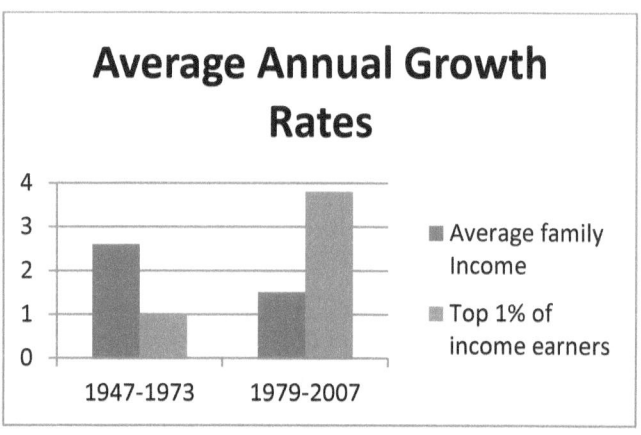

The effect of this income transformation has been staggering as suggested by the Paris School of Economics World Top Incomes Database. According to the data, the top 10% of income earners in the United States in 2008 control 48.2% of the wealth, up a staggering 13.6 percentage points since 1980. During the same period, the average gross income of the richest 1% of American households rose by 172% in real terms.[313]

This compares with the bottom 90% of American households, which rose by just 2% during the same period. In fact, if we look at the figures in real terms, we see that the average household income for the bottom 90% is actually lower in 2008 than it was in the early 1970s.[314]

It's all About the Share Price

As mentioned previously, businesses expect their share price to go up consistently, based on sound economic fundamentals. This is simply how business is supposed to work. But when this becomes the sole criteria upon which a company is measured, then it poses serious question on how it affects the very fabric of American society and indeed most other developed societies.

In November 2011, Professor Lynn Stout from UCLA gave her perspective on this subject, whilst in Sydney as a guest of the Centre for Law, Markets and Regulation at the Faculty of Law, UNSW. This is a précis of what she had to say.

Fifty years ago, senior executives ran their corporations with a view to benefiting not only the shareholders, but also their customers, employees and the larger society. Today most of that socially moral stance is largely non-existent. Through the beliefs of modern day journalists, academics and executives, the new ideology is to focus solely on the share price. The company, they claim, belongs to the shareholder and it appears that no-one else matters.

But the strategy is clearly failing. Because executives are focussed solely on raising the share price, many dubious decisions are made. In her own words, Lynn Stout stated;

"In the quest to "unlock shareholder value" they sell key assets, fire loyal employees and ruthlessly squeeze the workforce that remains; cut back on customer assistance and research and development; delay replacing outworn and unsafe equipment; shower executives with stock options to "incentivise" them; leverage firms until they teeter on the brink of insolvency; and lobby regulators to change the law so they can chase short-term profits speculating in high-risk financial derivatives."

Simply stated, the new shareholder ideology is just that – an ideology. It is not an aspect of corporate law in the United States, which requires directors of public corporations to maximise shareholder wealth. In fact the reverse is true. A legal doctrine called "the business judgement rule" mentions several other goals, including: expanding the firm, creating high-quality products, protecting employees and serving the public interest.

As Stout puts it, shareholder value is a managerial choice, not a legal requirement. She states that many shareholders are willing to sacrifice some profits to allow the company to act in an ethical and socially responsible fashion. Without taking steps in this regard, we run the risk of reducing our shareholders to the lowest common denominator.

One such example, where cost cutting took precedence over employees, the environment and the public at large, was the huge oil spill in 2010 in the Gulf of Mexico by BP. Not only did the spill cause enormous pain and suffering to the people and families, who lost their livelihood, but 11 workers died in the accident. Stout claims that BP's quest to "maximise shareholder value" proved to be disastrous.[315]

Perhaps the time has come for corporate leaders to revert back to the ethical days of fifty years ago. They can still have a focus on the share price, but not to the detriment of the rest of society.

Chapter 15

Disgraceful Executive Salaries

∞∞∞∞

As discussed in the previous chapter, the exponential rate of increase in executive salaries far outstripped the rate of increase of the average worker. This in itself is an indictment against the capitalist system, but it doesn't end there. In this chapter, we give examples of just how self-serving large corporates can be when it comes to looking after their own – and we are not talking about their workers. Here are a few examples.

The Airline Industry

In 2002, US Airlines CEO, Stephen Wolf, was given an executive payout of $15 million, six months before the airline filed for Chapter 11 bankruptcy. The airline survived, thanks to a government-guaranteed loan through the Air Transportation Stabilization Board. But, under the conditions of the bailout, the pilots' pension plans were terminated.[316]

In 2005, a federal judge in Chicago ruled that United Airlines could walk away from the $6.6 billion in retirement obligations to 119,000 current and former workers and handed the program to the federal Pensions Benefit Guaranty Corp, a government organisation that guarantees workers' pensions, but at a much lower rate.[317] But this decision didn't affect executive salaries. In 2011, United Airlines CEO, Jeffery Smisek, earned a staggering $13.4 million.[318]

In September 2005, two more airlines filed for Chapter 11 bankruptcy - Delta Airlines and Northwest Airlines. [319] In 2011, American Airlines also filed for bankruptcy protection under Chapter 11. There is no question that airlines have gone through difficult times since 911 and the global downturn in 2007-2008. Yet for a whole industry to be allowed to fail, speaks volumes about the quality of their executives and the management decisions that were taken during these difficult periods. So what is the price of failure that the CEOs have to bear?

In 2002, while Delta Airlines was losing $1.3 billion, its CEO, Leo Mullin received a massive $13 million. At the same time, 16,000 employees lost their jobs.[320] Interestingly, the CEO of Northwest Airlines from 2001-2004, Richard Anderson, is now CEO for Delta Airlines and is paid $8.3 million.[321] Also in 2002, Continental Airlines boss, received a total package of $11.9 million - double what he earned in the previous year, while the airline reported a $451 million dollar loss.[322] Other airline executives were also well-remunerated according to a Bloomberg News estimate. Bloomberg claims that Glenn Tilto of United Airlines received $24 million total compensation in 2006; Northwest's Doug Steenland received $26 million worth of shares; and US Airways Doug Parker got a $14 million package.[323] However, it should be mentioned that not all airline executives have feathered their own nests while the industry has been in trouble. American Airlines CEO and Chairman, Gerard Arpey resigned after 30 years, with a belief that bankruptcy was morally wrong. He left with no severance package and nearly worthless share options.[324] If only more executives would have the same moral standards.

The Finance Industry

Perhaps the area of executive salaries, which raises the ire of most Americans, is in the finance industry. In the year before the collapse of Lehman Bros in 2008, the top 50 employees had received bonuses of nearly $700 million. Yet the demise of Lehman Bros proved to be just the tip of the iceberg for the financial crisis meltdown. Between 2004 and 2007, the top five investment banks, having increased their financial leverage, reported a debt of over $4.1 trillion in fiscal year 2007 (about 30% of USA nominal GDP).[325]

From the top five investment banks, Lehman Bros was liquidated; Bear Sterns and Merrill Lynch were sold at highly discounted prices; and Goldman Sachs and Morgan Stanley became commercial banks, which subjected them to more stringent regulation. These last four companies all received government assistance.[326] So how did their executives fair, given the abject failure of their respective organisations?

The top five executives at Goldman Sachs earned $305 million.[327] Merrill Lynch's Chairman, Stan O'Neal retired after announcing an $8 billion loss, but still managed to obtain a final pay of $161 million.[328] Thomas Montag, head of Global Sales and Trading, was paid $39.4 million by Bank of America, which took over the struggling company. And this was after Merrill Lynch, the division that he ran, racked up the biggest share of the company's $15.3 billion net loss for Q4, 2008.[329]

The executives at Bear Stearns sold their company to JP Morgan Chase in 2008 for $2.00 a share, less than 10% of its value a week earlier and considerably less than $171 a share in January 2007. Although the company was a veritable basket case, their executives somehow escaped totally unscathed. The then CEO, James Cayne took out $156 million in total compensation from 2002 through 2006. The Current CEO, Schwartz made $141 million and former Co-President, Warren Spector, who was deposed after the hedge fund debacle earned $168 million.[330]

As for the ill-fated Lehman Bros, it was reported that senior executives and traders were paid between $8.2 million and $51.3 million in the year before the collapse. The same article claimed that 42 people were awarded at least $10 million. In total, 50 employees were awarded $700 million in that year.[331] Morgan Stanley CEO, John Mack, on the other hand, only received a modest $1.2 million.

In another Wall Street disgrace, Citigroup CEO, Chuck Prince oversaw multi-billion dollar write-downs, but still walked away with $38 million in bonuses, shares and stock options.[332]

No matter how we shake this up and analyse the results, it raises serious questions about how senior executives are rewarded. Looking at this tawdry list, it appears that many Wall Street executives are being paid extremely well for what can only be described as complete and utter failure. How was it possible that governments, shareholders and boards of directors allowed this to happen? The frightening aspect is that it seems we have not learned our lesson. The totally unjustified incomes of senior executives still continue today. Below is a list of America's top 10 executive salaries for the year 2011-2012.[333]

Top 10 Executive Salaries

No. 10: Michael Watford CEO:
Company: Ultra Petroleum (UPL)
Industry: Oil and natural gas
Compensation: $43.7 million

No. 9: John Wren CEO:
Company: Omnicom Group (OMC)
Industry: Advertising
Compensation: $45.6 million

No. 8: Stephen Hemsley CEO:
Company: UnitedHealth Group (UNH)
Industry: Health care plans
Compensation: $48.8 million

No. 7: Lew Frankfort CEO:
Company: Coach (COH)
Industry: Handbags, accessories
Compensation: $49.5 million

No. 6: Jeffrey Boyd CEO:
Company: Priceline.com (PCLN)

Industry: Travel services
Compensation: $50.2 million

No. 5: George Paz CEO:
Company: Express Scripts (ESRX)
Industry: Pharmacy benefit management
Compensation: $51.5 million

No. 4: Robert Iger CEO:
Company: Walt Disney (DIS)
Industry: Entertainment and media
Compensation: $53.3 million

No. 3: Michael Fascitelli CEO:
Company: Vornado Realty Trust (VNO)
Industry: Real estate investment trust
Compensation: $64.4 million

No. 2: Ralph Lauren CEO:
Company: Polo Ralph Lauren (RL)
Industry: Apparel
Compensation: $66.7 million

No. 1: John Hammergren CEO:
Company: McKesson (MCK)
Industry: Pharmaceuticals
Compensation: $131.2 million

Finally, we have one more example. In May 2012, the investment bank JP Morgan Chase registered a trading loss of

$2 billion through their London division. As a result, Ina Drew, JP Morgan's Chief Investment Officer, who oversaw the division, resigned her position. As a result of her obvious failure, she left with a miserable golden handshake of $32 million.[334] And one interesting note is the total absence of Wall Street executives in the top 10 salary earner's list. This is because the list only applies to publicly listed companies. If the salaries in the top 10 listed above, seem exorbitant, have a look at what's happening in the hedge fund business.

Hedge Funds

Hedge funds are private companies, which can take a wider range of investment activities than other funds. Their investors are typically institutions, such as pension funds, university endowments, foundations and high net worth individuals.[335] Two of their main strategies are short selling and leverage.

The problem with hedge funds, as seen by the general public, is that because they are private companies, they have few public disclosure requirements. This is sometimes seen as a lack of transparency.[336] There is also a public perception that hedge fund managers are not subject to the same regulatory oversight or registration requirements as other financial investment managers.

In spite of the collapse of the financial markets in 2007-2008, hedge fund managers still took home obscene amounts of money. In 2008, the top 25 managers reaped a total of $11.6 billion in pay.[337] Although this was around half of what they earned in 2007 ($22.5 billion), it must be remembered that 2008 was a year when losses were recorded at two out of three hedge funds. Yet the people in charge still managed to look after themselves. For example, James Simmons, from Renaissance Technologies, earned $2.5 billion; John Paulson, who made his fortune betting against the housing market, earned $2 billion and George Soros earned $1.1 billion.[338]

While they were feathering their own nest, millions of people in the United States and around the world watched in desperation as their property and share portfolios plummeted, leaving many penniless, homeless and hungry. Perhaps now, we can understand why the OWS protesters are so upset about the total inequity in our society. It is an indictment on a deregulated capitalist system and an indictment on the morality of the top 1% of money earners.

The Giving Pledge, a Ray of Hope

The fact that many executive business decisions are based solely on share price performance over the past few decades is no longer in question. Gone are the days when decisions were made solely in the interest of the public good. Also, the days when company loyalty was a two-way street appear to have been lost in the immoral scramble for greed.

But there is a ray of hope that some executives have "seen the light" and are making considerable contributions to improve the lives of many people, both at home and abroad. Whether it is as a result of feelings of guilt or a new found altruism is not really important. The fact is that many high-flying individuals are finding that their true calling in life is to help others.

Forbes magazine claimed that as at 2011, the United States had 413 billionaires, from all walks of life.[339] Collectively, their net worth is estimated to be around $1.53 trillion.[340] Until recently, there seemed to be only a small number of these billionaires, who had openly used their wealth for philanthropic purposes. There are probably two reasons for this. Many chose not to disclose how much money they were donating to charities and still many more had not yet given anything, perhaps waiting for a foundation to be created in their name, after they died. Whatever the reasons, the apparent lack of interest in philanthropy, stirred the two wealthiest Americans into action. With a combined net worth exceeding $100 billion,[341] Warren Buffet and Bill Gates launched the *Giving Pledge* campaign in June 2010.[342] By April 2012, the campaign had attracted some 81 billionaires, who have all pledged to donate at least half of their fortunes away to charity.[343]

One of the new additions to the growing list of contributors was Home Depot co-founder Arthur Blank. On his *Giving Pledge*, Blank wrote;

"The needs in our society are more profound than at any point in my lifetime. The gap between rich and poor in America is growing. Philanthropy alone cannot repair all of the social injustice in our country or the world. It can, however, inspire good will, spark innovation and provide thought leadership."[344]

There are many notable names that are on the list and one can only hope that most of the 400+ American billionaires will find it in their hearts to commit to this fine social concept. One noteworthy addition to *Giving Pledge* was Facebook co-founder Mark Zuckerberg, who signed up in December 2010. Please refer to the endnote for a complete list of billionaires, who have committed to the *Giving Pledge* as at 30th June 2012.[345]

Chapter 16

The End of Capitalism?

∞∞∞∞

In the past, capitalism has served the West reasonably well. During most of the 20th century, it has continued to survive even through the most difficult times, such as the two World Wars and the Great Depression. The only alternative to capitalism, if you listened to the propaganda, was communism. But Marxist-Leninist communism was doomed for failure as witnessed by the collapse of the Soviet Union in the late 1980s. At the time, capitalism reigned supreme and the old enemy, communism, was dead and buried, except of course for a few countries, which resisted western based economics; countries such as China, Vietnam, North Korea and Cuba, the last two of which are economic basket cases.

With communism out of the way, capitalism was free to do as it wished, as long as it remained unregulated. The results of this unconstrained freedom soon became a freight train running out of control. As discussed in previous chapters, corporate coffers and executive salaries started increasing exponentially at the cost of social benefits, the environment, the betterment of humanity and the forgotten 99%.

Globalisation and free trade agreements became the new buzzwords from economists as they promised to deliver a fairer share to those who most need a helping hand. It was the system that could eliminate poverty, particularly in Africa and Asia, by making food and commodities more affordable. But it wasn't just corporate executives who benefited from this over-indulgence. Hollywood actors, sports stars, TV and radio personalities all jumped on the bandwagon, with salaries and pay packages that could never be justified. And it was all as a result of the "greed is good" philosophy.

High flyers were rewarded even further by paying lower taxes, due to a number of tax concessions for the wealthy. But it didn't take long for the big boys to get even greedier. It was no longer about the money. After all, how many millions of dollars does one need? It was always about power. Corporate politics entered into a dog eat dog world. If you didn't grow, you would be taken over. And this is what capitalism is really all about. Capitalism cannot survive without growth. Annual GDP is how we measure the health of a nation. On average, 3% growth per year seems to be a healthy growth rate for most western nations.

The problem with this scenario is that growth can only come from two sources – increased consumption or increased population. But unfettered growth cannot continue on indefinitely. If world GDP continues at 3% per annum, then we will be doubling our consumption every 24 years.[346] Put in another way, in 100 years, we will be consuming 16 times the amount of the earth's resources as we are today. Humanity cannot survive under this system. We are running out of oil, fresh water and food. Rainforests the size of the Costa Rica, are being destroyed every year[347] and global warming, a consequence of a runaway capitalist system is fast reaching a tipping point, beyond which there will be no return.

During the past 100 years, the world's population has increased from 2 billion to 7 billion people. While this may have been a boon to capitalism, it has resulted in the near devastation of the earth's environment and a rapid depletion of our natural resources. It is clear that this exponential population growth cannot continue indefinitely. Whether the world's population can stabilise before a catastrophic depression occurs, is yet to be determined.

There are many scholars and economists who are now questioning the wisdom of unregulated capitalism, based on the free market system and globalisation. Even the International Monetary Fund (IMF), which once preached the promotion of free markets and less government, has changed its tune, since the advent of the Global Financial Crisis (GFC). Just before their annual meeting in Washington, in 2008, Dominique Strauss-Kahn, the Managing Director of the IMF stated;

"Obviously the crisis comes from an important regulatory and supervisory failure in advanced countries . . . and a failure in market discipline mechanics."[348]

After the GFC hit, the President of the World Bank, Robert Zoellick, was asked whether it was in the developing world's interest to continue embracing the free-market reforms of the developed world. He replied that he thought there was much confusion about the free-market in both the developing and the developed world, as a result of the GFC.[349]

During the past 30 years, the United States has been instrumental in spruiking the benefits of the American global economic model. It believed that the only way forward for developing countries was to rid the finance industry from government regulation. But this self-regulatory approach is being blamed for the easy credit that caused a collapse in the housing market and allowed an out-of-control Wall Street to create toxic investments on the international financial system.

Joseph Stiglitz, the Nobel Prize-winning economist from Columbia University summed up the situation this way;

"People around the world once admired us for our economy, and we told them if you wanted to be like us, here's what you have to do - hand over power to the market. The point now is that no one has respect for that kind of model anymore given this crisis. And of course it raises questions about our credibility. Everyone feels they are suffering now because of us."

The collapse of the free-market system has its detractors overseas as well. A case in point is from South Korea. After the Korean War, South Korea adopted most of the free market principles, while North Korea remained a communist state ruled by a dictator. The differences between the two economies couldn't be clearer. Since the war, South Korea's economy has grown substantially by following the American model. But they are now very sceptical about the excesses this model has produced. Kang Man-soo, the South Korean Finance Minister said;

"Derivatives and hedge funds are like casino gambling. A lot of Koreans are asking, how can the United States be so weak?" [350]

Perhaps the most damning criticism of the free-market system comes from Charlie Munger, a long-time business partner of Warren Buffet, one of America's richest men. Munger put it as plain as one can;

"It's over for America. Yes, o-v-e-r. America's in decline, at the end-of-days, coming to financial ruin." [351]

Munger also wrote a parable about how one nation, named "Basicland" came to financial ruin. The parable is about America and is entitled *"Basically It's Over"*. Without going into the details of the story, listed below are the titles of the 10 scenes, which make up the parable.[352]

- Scene 1: Power and wealth create false sense of invincibility
- Scene 2: Greed consumes America: Gambling replaces real work
- Scene 3: Wall Street's casinos prosper as Main Street suffers
- Scene 4: America's side-bet debt to foreign casinos skyrockets

- Scene 5: Nations in denial rarely prepare for disasters in advance
- Scene 6: In the later stages, get-rich-quick beats real work
- Scene 7: Wall Street CEOs, economists, lobbyists love gambling
- Scene 8: Wall Street gamblers love Reaganomics, hate change
- Scene 9: Main Street investors join Wall Street's 'Happy Conspiracy'
- Scene 10: Politicians love Wall Street's derivative casino: Game over!

Whether this doomsday scenario plays out will be dependent on how much the United States is prepared to put ethics and government controls back into the American financial system. Wall Street and Government must accept the error of its ways and make major changes to regulate the financial system, which has an out-of-control addiction to gambling.

It took less than 200 years for the United Kingdom to fall from superpower to also-rans. Given the speed of change that we are currently witnessing, the reign of the United States as the dominant superpower is fast coming to a close. Capitalism is not a perfect system, but it's streets ahead of Communism. However, if it is to succeed in some form in the future, then massive action must be taken to eliminate the processes that caused the GFC in 2007-2008. If politicians fail to learn from the sins of the past, when it comes to ethics and capitalism, then capitalism is sure to fail and when it does, it will mark the demise of a once great nation, which could have a domino effect for the rest of the developed world.

America's Lost Morality

Part III

American Government's Lost Morality

Foreign Affairs

America's Lost Morality

Chapter 17

The Middle East

∞∞∞∞

All western governments have alliances with other countries, which provide mutual support against wilful aggression by other nations. These alliances are often supported by an official treaty, such as with the ANZUS alliance or the NATO alliance. No-one would argue against these partnerships, which are designed to safeguard their sovereignty and independence, simply through their existence. It's a form of solidarity that has stood the test of time well.

Even non-western nations have similar agreements in place; the Arab League is one that is becoming more prominent. The challenge comes when decisions are made on the basis of political expediency, especially when these decisions are unsupported by world opinion.

A case in point is the unqualified support that the United States has had for Israel and its struggle with the Palestinians. The reason for this support is absolutely clear. No political party in the United States could survive without the support of the powerful Jewish lobby. At first glance, this is perfectly acceptable. After all, this is what politics is all about. Politicians do everything in their power to persuade most minority groups to vote for their political party. So what is the problem with this rationale?

The main problem is that by overtly supporting Israel in order to secure their votes at home, the United States has willingly or otherwise, marginalised the lives of 4.4 million Palestinians. Most political observers would agree that the Palestinians have just as much right to a homeland and political independence as the Israelis. But this can only occur if the United States takes a more considered and balanced approach in the long-standing Middle East conflict.

Let's take one example. On 29th November 1947, the United Nations General Assembly voted in favour of creating independent Arab and Jewish states in Palestine. The vote was 33 for, 13 against, 10 abstentions and 1 absent.[353] Interestingly, for the vote to have been passed required a two thirds majority, not counting abstaining and absent members. The vote, if held when originally planned on 26th November 1947 would have failed.[354]

At the time, the Palestinian Arabs and other Arab nations were opposed to the separation because Jews made up only 33% of the population. There can be no question that the non-acceptance of the agreement by the Arab community has led to wars and political unrest ever since. This fact was acknowledged by Palestinian president Mahmoud Abbas in 2011; a situation he was trying to rectify.[355]

Nevertheless, subsequent disclosures indicate that the vote was not entirely "kosher." President Truman noted afterwards:

"The facts were that not only were there pressure movements around the United Nations unlike anything that had been seen there before, but that the White House, too, was subjected to a constant barrage. I do not think I ever had as much pressure and propaganda aimed at the White House as I had in this instance. The persistence of a few of the extreme Zionist leaders—actuated by political motives and engaging in political threats—disturbed and annoyed me."[356]

At the same time, Liberia's Ambassador to the United States complained that the US delegation threatened aid cuts to several countries, including their own.[357] But one of the most interesting cases was how the Philippine government was coerced to change its vote.

In the days before the vote, the Philippines' representative General Carlos P. Romulo stated;

"We hold that the issue is primarily moral. The issue is whether the United Nations should accept responsibility for the enforcement of a policy which is clearly repugnant to the valid nationalist aspirations of the people of Palestine. The Philippines Government holds that the United Nations ought not to accept such responsibility".

After a phone call from Washington, the representative was recalled and the Philippines' vote changed in favour of the Zionists.[358] Further pressure was placed on wavering nations by a group of 26 American senators with influence on foreign aid bills that sent a telegram to wavering countries, seeking their support for the partition plan.

Most people would agree that this type of heavy-handed political pressure occurs all the time – after all moral politics is considered to be an oxymoron. But let's skip forward some 64 years, when Palestine attempted to get United Nations recognition for a Palestinian statehood.

On 18th January 2012, 130 countries or 67.4% of the United Nations member states voted to recognise the State of Palestine.[359] This represented 80% of the world's population. Yet, Israel, with continued unfettered support from the United States, still illegally occupies many of the territories it captured during the 1967 war. Jewish settlements are continuing to be built and "legalised" by the Israeli government. As at January 2012, Israel has established about 150 settlements in the West Bank, including East Jerusalem, in addition to about 100 "outposts" erected by settlers without official authorization.[360]

The settler population is estimated at approximately at 500,000, the United Nations Office for the Coordination of Humanitarian Affairs said.[361] So, how can these highly illegal and immoral acts keep on happening? The answer is simple. They could not happen without the complete support of the United States government. The total disregard for the social, humanitarian and political needs of the Palestinian people have been completely and deliberately ignored. One only has to look at a few facts to come to this conclusion. In Fig 17.1, we can see how Israel has continued to encroach into Palestinian territory, between 1946 and 2000. This would not have happened without the unqualified support of the United States.

Fig. 17.1 (Israeli expansion into Occupied Territories)

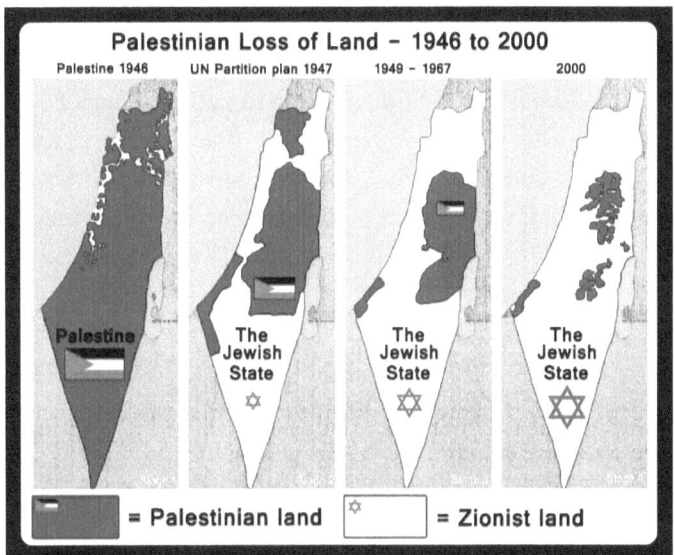

Perhaps the most outstanding feature of the self-righteous attitude that the United States has taken over the years in the Israeli-Palestinian conflict, can be seen through the offices of the United Nations Security Council. Between 1972 and early 2011, the United States exercised its veto right 42 times on UN resolutions critical of Israel.[362] On each occasion, theirs was the only veto cast. Despite the fact that all other members of the Security Council were either in favour or abstained, this blatant abuse of power by the United States has been allowed to continue with total impunity, to the detriment of the Palestinian people. A complete list of these vetos can be found at the website in the endnote.[363]

One can only speculate whether the current wave of Islamist radicalism against the West, could have been reduced or even negated had the United States taken more of a neutral stance in Middle East politics. There can be no question that Israel could not have continued with its illegal and indiscriminate land grab in the West Bank without the support of the United States.

To add credence to this statement, we only have to examine the amount of military aid that is going to both countries in the conflict. In the fiscal year 2011, the United States provided Israel with at least $8.2 million *each day* in military aid while the Palestinians received $0.[364] Total direct aid to Israel has amounted to well over $140 billion since 1976. Since 1994, the Palestinian Authority has received $3.3 billion in non-military aid.[365] This compares to $6.5 billion in non-military aid to Israel between 2001 and 2010.[366]

It can be argued that the United States has every right to provide aid to any country, to which it sees fit. This is, without question, the prerogative of any sovereign nation. However, given the sensitivity of the Israeli-Palestinian conflict, the United States has been out of step with world opinion. This is clearly evident by the intransigent positions it has taken through the use of their veto power in the United Nations Security Council.

Is it possible that these actions resulted in widespread Islamic animosity towards the United States and its Western allies? If we step into the shoes of the Palestinian people for a moment, would we not feel oppressed? Could not these feelings transform into acts of desperation against the aggressors?

There can be no question that the atrocities of 911 and other similar attacks around the world could never be justified, no matter how difficult it has been for the Palestinian people. But we need to ask, could these atrocities have been avoided if the United States had taken a more balanced view of world opinion, instead of simply trying to satisfy the Jewish lobby for political reasons?

Perhaps the real solution to this moral dilemma is for the United Nations to completely ban the power of the veto. Then maybe, for the first time since its inception, we will see true democracy in action, where every vote has an equal value. Imagine what the world might have been like, if the veto had not been incorporated into the UN Charter. However, this was never likely to happen. As president Truman stated in his memoirs;

> "All our experts, civil and military, favored it, and without such a veto no arrangement would have passed the Senate."[367]

It appears, yet again, that the moral and social well-being of the majority of nations in the world was sacrificed for the self-interest of the United States. True democracy, it seems, exists in name only.

Chapter 18

War, Torture and Rendition

∞∞∞

A ny nation has the right to defend itself when there is an attack on its sovereign territory, such as what happened to the United States, when Japan attacked Pearl Harbor on 7th December 1941. This is usually done with a "Declaration of War" against the enemy, but in the United States, this has happened only five times since the adoption of the Constitution in 1789. However, since the end of World War II, there have been four separate occasions when the United States went to war illegally, without Congressional approval; in Korea 1950-53, Vietnam 1966-75, Afghanistan 2001-present and Iraq 2002-2011. On several other occasions, the military was used for shorter conflicts in Libya - 1986, Panama – 1989, Iraq – 1991, Somalia – 1992, Bosnia – 1995, Kosovo – 1999 and Libya 2011.[368]

Not one of these conflicts could be justified as an act of self-defence, based on an attack on US territory by a foreign state. Some would argue that 911 was such an attack, thereby justifying the 2001 incursion into Afghanistan. Yet when we look at the terrorists, 15 came from Saudi Arabia, 2 from the UAR and 1 each from Lebanon and Egypt,[369] yet none of these countries were attacked. I am certain that arguments will prevail for decades to come, over the perceived legitimacy of the attack on Afghanistan, based on the belief that was where Osama bin Laden was hiding. Even so, one would have to draw a long bow to justify an attack on another sovereign nation, after such a terrorist attack. What if bin Laden was known to be hiding in Saudi Arabia, where he was born? Would the United States have invaded Saudi Arabia? Given their vast quantities of oil reserves and their close ties with the US, it is highly unlikely that any such attack would have occurred.

These acts of aggression against other sovereign states were not only illegal, they were highly immoral. Let's have a look at the real reasons for these incursions, in each of the major wars, listed above.

Korea

World War II had ended and the cold war had begun; a war that would continue for over 40 years. Korea became a pawn in an ideological chess game between western democracies (capitalism) and eastern communism. At the end of World War II, Korea was still being ruled by Japan, as it had done since 1910. When Japan lost the war, Korea was split into two parts. The USSR would control the north and the United States would control the south, separated at the 38th parallel.[370]

The ideological cold war accelerated rapidly when China became the world's most populous communist nation in October 1949. President Truman's main concern was that other countries around China might also become communist, such as Japan. He had also just finished investing a large amount of money in the American military and he felt that Americans wanted to see this new army in action. Their confidence was high after the devastating defeat of Japan a few years earlier and they saw the spread of communism as being against American democratic principles. To add to this, the United Nations had just been created and it desperately needed to stamp its authority and influence on world affairs, else it could meet the same fate as its predecessor, the failed League of Nations.

Kim Il-Sung, who had been installed as leader of North Korea by the USSR, decided that the people of the south would be better off under his leadership. On 25th June 1950, he invaded South Korea and pushed deep into South Korean Territory. A month later, the United Nations Army intervened and successfully pushed the North Koreans back close to the Chinese border. China issued a warning to the United Nations to pull back to the 38th parallel, but this was ignored.[371]

It was at this point that the head of the United Nations forces, General McArthur, had two choices. He could have heeded the warning and use his act of good faith as a basis for crisis talks with North Korea and China. Instead, he chose war. As a result of this lost opportunity for dialog with the perceived enemy, the United Nations, with massive support from America decided that trying to attain an ideological victory was worth the cost of war. Neither side could have predicted the disastrous result that followed. According to some estimates, 36,516 Americans lost their lives.[372] It is also estimated that over 900 thousand North Koreans and up to 2 million civilians lost their lives in the three year conflict[373] - and for what purpose? The war ended in a stalemate with no peace being declared. To this day, North Korea is still separated from South Korea at the 38th parallel – the same dividing line that was suggested by China in October 1950. Yet, it took less than four months for the United States to forget the lessons learned from this tragic and highly immoral war. By November 1953, they were indirectly involved in their next shameful and illegal war – Vietnam

Vietnam

In fact, the United States first became involved in 1950, when President Truman approved $10 million in military assistance in an attempt to thwart the communist thrust into Indochina.[374] At the time, the French were the effective government of Indochina and the money was used to purchase military equipment to be used against the communist Viet Minh. In 1951, a further $150 million worth of support was authorised by President Truman.[375] But it was in 1953 that American C-119 aircraft were loaned to the French Commander, General Navarre. At first, these aircraft were flown by French pilots, but only until 1954, when the United States CIA started flying the aircraft undercover, using the French insignia.[376] However, this was not enough to defeat the determined Viet Minh. The battle of Dien Bien Phu ended in the defeat of the French, leading to a negotiated settlement, which would see Vietnam divided into north and south, until democratic elections could be held in 1956.[377] But these elections never occurred.

Although the French agreed to relinquish sovereignty over Vietnam, Laos and Cambodia, they, along with the United States, refused to sign the Geneva Accord. Instead, in

September 1954, the United States, together with Australia, France, Great Britain, New Zealand, Pakistan, the Philippines, and Thailand, formed the Southeast Asia Treaty Organization (SEATO), which sole purpose was to resist the spread of communism in Southeast Asia.[378] Clearly, this was another example of the United States putting their anti-communist ideology ahead of what would become yet another illegal war that was destined for failure. But President Eisenhower's fear of the spread of communism, in what he described as the "domino principle" prevailed; the consequences of which were catastrophic. While the list of casualties varies significantly, depending on the source, it is still a massively devastating total. The list reads as follows: American military – 58,272;[379] South Vietnam military – in excess of 250 thousand;[380] North Vietnam military and Viet Cong – in excess of 1 million;[381] civilians – up to 4 million on both sides.[382]

The war ended in 1975, when the North Vietnamese Army captured Saigon. The United States sponsored SEATO had been defeated. There were so many casualties, so many wounded and so many families destroyed as a result of this conflict; all of which could have been avoided, if the United States agreed to sign the Geneva Accord. It was another example of its "might is right" philosophy. Unfortunately one can only conclude that when there is a conflict between morality and ideology, then ideology will win out every time. The question must be asked; how many more lives must be needlessly sacrificed before we put an end to unjustified wars?

Afghanistan

The immensity of the tragedy that struck the United States on 911 cannot be understated. The nation, as well as the rest of the civilised world, was in total shock. There was no question that some form of massive retaliation was required, if the United States were to maintain its dignity and self-esteem. But was the invasion of Afghanistan seriously flawed from a legal perspective? The United Nations Charter, which was signed by all the participating coalition countries, states that all members must settle their disputes peacefully and that the use of military force is not to be used, except for the purposes of self-defence. As a consequence, the United Nations Security Council did not authorise the military campaign in Afghanistan.[383]

The United States, in clear disregard for the United Nations Charter, claimed that it did not require Security Council authorisation, because the invasion was an act of self-defence and not a war of aggression. But critics of this stance firmly disagreed, stating that the invasion of Afghanistan was not an act of self-defence because attacks were not "armed attacks" by another state, but rather conducted by individuals, none of whom had any proven connection to Afghanistan.

The end result was a lengthy and costly war that could never be won and could never be justified. In the process, the coalition had 2,853 casualties by 3rd March 2012.[384] Estimates of civilian casualties range from 17,000 to 37,000,[385] and the total operational cost to the end of fiscal year 2011 was $468 billion. [386] The main target of the invasion, Osama bin Laden, was finally killed by a secret US military incursion into

Pakistan in 2011. Even this was conducted without the permission of their ally, the Pakistani government.

Iraq

In 2003, President Bush authorised yet another illegal war; this time against Iraq. It was based on some trumped up charge that Saddam Hussein was harbouring weapons of mass destruction (WMD); a claim that later proved to be false.

The war, which was not sanctioned by the United Nations, was generally not supported by the American public. In a CBS poll, taken in January 2003, 63% wanted Bush to seek a diplomatic solution rather than engaging in yet another war, while 62% felt that the threat of terrorism against the US would increase as a result of going to war.[387] Even some of its strongest traditional allies, such as France, Germany, Canada and New Zealand opposed the war. The very thought of another war triggered world-wide condemnation. One estimate indicated that over 36 million people took part in over 3000 protests across the globe, between 3rd January and 12th April 2003.[388]

But this was ignored by the self-righteous neo-cons in Washington and the "might is right" principle was applied once more. Congress overwhelmingly supported the invasion of Iraq on the basis that it was the policy of the United States to remove Saddam Hussein and to promote a democratic replacement. But before the end of 2003, many respected organisations, including the International Commission of Jurists and the US-based Lawyers Committee on Nuclear Policy, had proclaimed the invasion to be illegal. Even one of Bush's administrators, Richard Perle, conceded that the invasion was illegal.[389]

In the opinion of many, the war was completely avoidable and totally unnecessary. It went against all International agreements, including the United Nations Charter and the United States Constitution. And, as it was with the three previously-mentioned wars, the human and monetary costs were excessive. Over 100,000 civilians were killed and nearly 4,500 American forces lost their lives.[390] The true financial cost of the war is estimated by some to be in excess of $3 trillion.[391]

Considering there are many other countries that are led by dictators, one has to ask; why was it so imperative to get rid of Saddam Hussein? After all, North Korea is a dictatorship *and* has weapons of mass destruction. Many articles have been written that support the view that the only reason is that Iraq has oil and North Korea does not. Whatever the real reasons, there can be no doubt that the United States will do anything, even sacrificing the lives of their own soldiers, to ensure their economy is not eroded by realistic or perceived threats, such as higher fuel prices. Once again, it appears that morality is not always in the psyche of the American political machine.

However, before we close on the subject of the morality in foreign affairs, there is one more aspect that needs to be discussed.

Rendition and Torture

The 26th June 1987 is the date that the *United Nations Convention against Torture* came into effect.[392] The

Convention, which has been signed by 147 countries, including the United States, as at September 2010,[393] states the following:

> Any act by which severe pain or suffering, whether physical or mental, is intentionally inflicted on a person for such purposes as obtaining from him or a third person, information or a confession, punishing him for an act he or a third person has committed or is suspected of having committed, or intimidating or coercing him or a third person, or for any reason based on discrimination of any kind, when such pain or suffering is inflicted by or at the instigation of or with the consent or acquiescence of a public official or other person acting in an official capacity. It does not include pain or suffering arising only from, inherent in or incidental to lawful sanctions.[394]

This extract is perfectly clear and there can be no ambiguity, whatsoever. Yet, when President Bush and Vice President Cheney secretly commenced a rendition and torture policy after 911, they were in fact choosing to ignore International agreements, to which the United States was a signatory. Furthermore, it could be argued that it was totally against accepted American standards and moral values.

The process of rendition and torture raises a number of serious questions. How could a supposedly moral society allow this to happen in the first place? How is it, despite its illegality, that no-one has ever been prosecuted for these atrocities? Is there one rule for those in power and another for everyone else? Imagine if an individual took it upon himself to subject someone to waterboarding, whom he perceived as being a threat to his family? Regardless of his personal beliefs, I am certain that he would be tried, convicted and incarcerated for a very long time.

Since 911, the CIA have captured an estimated 3,000 people and transported them around the world, in the name of "extraordinary rendition."[395] The justification for the process was to arrest and detain foreign nationals, who were regarded as suspected terrorists, and to transport them to foreign countries for further interrogation, without the need for public scrutiny.[396] According to one CIA official;

"The whole idea [becomes] a corruption of renditions. It's not rendering to justice, it's kidnapping."[397]

However, the United States did not act on its own. Many of the countries, to which the suspects were sent, are known for their human rights violations; countries such as Egypt, Syria, Jordan, Saudi Arabia and Morocco. This is ironic, if not hypocritical; given the United States' record of condemning human rights abuses in other countries, such as in the People's Republic of China.

To fully understand what is meant by "torture", we need only refer to the State Department's annual Human Rights report in 2001, when referring to Jordan, one of the participants in the scheme stated;

"The most frequently alleged methods of torture include sleep deprivation, beatings on the soles of the feet, prolonged suspension with ropes in contorted positions, and extended solitary confinement."

US officials are quoted as calling Jordan's interrogators "highly professional."[398] Then of course, there is the infamous waterboarding technique that was used.

It was not until 2007 that the CIA admitted to the use of this method of torture on extrajudicial prisoners; a procedure that had been authorised by the Department of justice.[399] US Government officials, at the time, did not think that waterboarding was a form of torture. So much so, Vice President Dick Cheney stated at a National Press Club address that, "I am a strong believer. I thought it was well done."[400] There was no question that the Bush administration was firmly in the belief that they had done nothing illegal by using waterboarding as an interrogation technique.

Unfortunately, they all conveniently chose not to recall the fact that the United States hung Japanese soldiers for waterboarding US prisoners-of-war on American soldiers during World War II.[401] This is yet another example of the double standards, which has allowed American morality to deteriorate since the middle of last century. The resultant abuse has severely diminished America's credibility, in the eyes of the rest of the world.

Part IV

American Government's Lost Morality

Domestic and Judicial

America's Lost Morality

Chapter 19

The American Tea Party

∞∞○∞

In 2010, the success of the Tea Party movement in America became headline news around the world. To American conservative republicans, it hailed a new beginning for their push for smaller government and the implementation of fundamental libertarian philosophies. To the rest of the world, they were perceived as an extension of the Bush era neo-conservatism at best, but largely, they were considered to be right-wing extremists, whose political platform was both naïve and lacking in credibility.

Many western democracies view American politics in an election year, as the longest-running and most expensive three ring circus on the planet. Add to that bizarre spectacle, the advent of the Tea Party, and we have an interesting, divisive and some would say potentially dangerous period ahead in American and world politics.

So what exactly is the Tea Party and what do they stand for? Who supports them and what is their typical demographic?

More importantly, what effect does their political philosophy have on morality, both locally and globally?

After viewing many documentaries and news articles on the Tea Party movement across America, particularly before the mid-term elections in 2010, the first thing that one notices is the almost complete absence of African-Americans, Latinos or any other ethnic minorities in their promotional rallies. To non-Americans, the Tea Party ideology seems to attract the most radical elements in American society; the Christian right, white supremacist groups, southern rednecks and National Rifle Association advocates, to name a few. Some would even consider them to be racists. This is despite the fact that Herman Cain, an African-American author, radio host and business executive, was an ardent supporter of the Tea Party movement. For a brief period, Cain was a candidate for the 2012 US Republican Party presidential nomination.[402]

In order to determine whether these criticisms are fair and just, we need to first look why the Tea Party was formed and exactly what they stand for. Only then can we begin to understand which elements of American society would most likely be attracted to their philosophy.

The Tea Party's main platform includes: less government spending;[403] opposition to taxation in varying degrees;[404] reduction of national debt and federal budget;[405] and strict adherence to the United States Constitution.[406] According to several polls, Tea party supporters are mainly white married males over 45 and are more conservative than the general public. This is backed up by the Bloomberg National Poll of adults, which showed that 40% of Tea party supporters are 55

170

or older, 79% are white, 61% are men and 44% identify themselves as "born again Christians".[407]

Given this particular demographic, one might easily conclude that their collective moral standards would be somewhat higher than the national average, accepting that statistics of this nature are difficult to quantify. So the question remains; Do the philosophy and policies of the Tea Party reflect the moral standards of its supporters? The answer might seem to be surprising, to all but the most faithful of Tea Party supporters.

To begin with, we need to examine some of the policies in more detail, some of which are listed above. In an article posted in the Tea Party Journal, the following claim is made:

Recognizing the inherent morality of free market capitalism means to first believe in its core values: maximized individual liberty, the opportunity for unlimited success and prosperity, and the goodness of failure.[408]

This sounds innocent enough on the surface, but there is a major flaw with this assumption. The thought that free market capitalism is "inherently moral" may make for a nice feel good slogan, but in reality, falls far short of the mark, as discussed in quite some detail in Part 2 of *America's Lost Morality*. In these chapters, we examined the many moral issues concerning the deregulated capitalist system and the role it played in conjunction with Big Oil, Big Tobacco, Big Pharmaceuticals, Agriculture, Wall Street and others. Contrary to Tea Party rhetoric, free market capitalism is not considered to be "inherently moral" by many observers. In fact there is a growing groundswell of public opinion that free market capitalism is morally bankrupt.

Another tenet in the Tea Party platform is the strict adherence to the United States Constitution. Again, this simplistic view seems to tug at the heartstrings of most Americans, regardless of their political allegiances. After all, the Constitution is the cornerstone of what the United States is all about, right? As an outside observer, it is clear that some aspects of the Constitution, which was written over 200 years ago, do not necessarily apply to today's world. One example can be taken from the Second Amendment with regard to the right to gun ownership. According to the National Rifle Association:

> NRA continues its mission to uphold Second Amendment rights and to advocate enforcement of existing laws against violent offenders to reduce crime.[409]

It is no secret that the majority of NRA's 4 million members support the policies of the Tea Party and they believe they have a Constitutional right to bear arms. This may have been acceptable 200 years ago, but it is no longer morally acceptable today. As discussed in Chapter 1, in the United States 10.27 people per 100,000 are killed by guns every year.[410] This compares with .07 per 100,000 in Japan,[411] a country that does not have a gun culture supported by a Constitution.

A third tenet of the Tea party platform is the opposition to taxation in varying degrees. But Bruce Bartlett from Forbes claims that "For an anti-tax group, they don't know much about taxes."[412] Apart from this and other criticisms, one wonders whether the Tea Party faithful have done their homework on taxation. Without taxation, there would be no schools, no hospitals, no police departments, no fire departments, no armed forces and no safety net for the poor, incapacitated and unemployed. Infrastructure such as electricity generation, water, gas, sewage, roads and bridges would not exist. The "taxed enough already" mantra may win support from the ignorant and naïve party faithful, but it has no moral credibility.

So just how much tax is enough to pay for all these services? What a person perceives and what is the reality may be quite different. Here are some facts to consider. At a Tea Party meeting on 16th March 2010 on Capitol Hill, Washington, approximately 15% of the demonstrators were asked two questions on tax revenues. Their answers were quite surprising, however, it should be noted that not everyone would be familiar with the true figures.

The first question concerned the size of government. They were asked how much the federal government receives in taxes as a percentage of gross domestic product (GDP). The Tea Party demonstrators came up with an average figure of 42% of GDP, with the median figure at 40%.[413] In fact, the highest figure since 1970 was 20.6% of GDP in 2000. The highest ever recorded was in 1944, which was at 20.9%.

The next question asked was how much tax would a person on an income of $50,000 pay each year. Again, their answers were a long way from the truth. The average response was $12,710 with a median of $10,000. In fact, according to calculations by the Joint Committee on Taxation, tax payers on an income of between $40,000 and $50,000 had an average federal tax burden of just 1.7%. This figure, however, did take into consideration the personal exemption of $3,600 and the standard deduction for single and married people, which is $5,700 and $11,400 respectively, at that time.[414]

So how can it be that Tea Party supporters have such a distorted view of taxation reality? Well, two things come to mind. First, we could not expect people from any political persuasion to have an in depth understanding of the taxation system. It is possible, for example that a similar result could be achieved from a sample of Occupy Wall Street supporters. Second – and here is where the morality issue comes in – the *leaders* of the Tea Party movement all know the truth about tax revenues, but if they chose to enlighten their followers with the facts, the movement may have died a political death before it got started. It is much better to keep them in the dark on the subject and stir up emotions with urban myths that seem to have their geneses in political rallies. It is a political example of the old management "mushroom theory". (If you are unfamiliar with this theory, please Google it.)

However, by far the most disturbing aspect of the Tea Party movement is its almost unqualified support from white evangelicals. In a survey by the Pew Research Center, five times as many white evangelicals supported the doctrine of the Tea Party as those that did not.[415] For minority groups, including black Protestants, Jewish, unaffiliated, atheist and agnostics, the reverse is true. In many ways this is as much an indictment against the religious right as it is against the policies of the Tea Party. How can it be that people of such strong religious conviction can support a political party, which is so deficient in social values? Is it not the role of religious

174

organisations to provide support, hope, kindness and compassion to those less fortunate?

As discussed earlier, the Tea Party stands for lower taxes and smaller government. This may sound like a grand ideological mantra to their supporters, but how can these policies help the unemployed, the sick and the needy? How many people have to become unemployed or lose their homes because of the actions of a view privileged business tycoons who care more for their shareholders' interests that those of their employees? How many people have to suffer in pain and alone because they cannot afford medical insurance? How many people have to live on the streets and beg for handouts because of the lack of social support? The Tea Party would argue that many of these issues can be addressed by voluntary social organisations, such as various church groups. But these groups have been around for centuries and the problem is getting worse. Much more support needs to come from governments at all levels and this means taxes must be raised for the wealthiest 1%, who just happens to own nearly 40% of the total wealth in the United States. A survey mentioned by Ron Paul, a strong Tea Party advocate, indicated that 10% of US citizens own 80% of the wealth.[416]In another survey, it was shown that the bottom 80% of the citizens own just 7% of the wealth.[417]

In 2005, a randomly selected sample of 5,522 people in the United States, were shown two pie charts of wealth distribution in the United States and in Sweden. The names of the countries were not shown and the single question that was asked was; in which country would you rather live? Before looking at the respondents' answers, it is important to look at the two countries' statistics. In the US the richest 20% were shown to own 84% of the wealth, whereas in Sweden, the richest 20% own just 36% of the wealth. Without knowing which pie chart belonged to which country, the respondents voted a staggering 92% in favour of the Swedish model.[418]

This only goes to prove that there is a wide discrepancy between the aspirations of the Tea Party and its supporters and the reality of what is happening in the United States today. The fact that these statistics are not largely known or understood is a disgrace. It is just another example as to how political parties can distort the facts and supress the truth in order to enhance their political power. It is clear that most Americans would prefer to live in a more egalitarian society, such as enjoyed by Sweden, often described as a popular socialist country. In America, socialism is a dirty word. It is often talked about with the same distaste as communism; a legacy of cold war propaganda. But nothing could be further from the truth.

According to David Dietz, a graduate from Georgetown University;

"Along with the rest of Scandinavia, Sweden is among the leaders in terms of quality of life,[419] enjoys one of the world's highest GDPs[420] and not surprisingly, continually ranks as having the happiest people on the planet."[421]

Sadly, the extreme political Right in the United States, led by the Tea Party, continue to prey on the ignorance of their supporters by using one line slogans, which denigrate the philosophy of socialism as being anti-American. Paul Froese from USA Today writes about his understanding of the subject.

"Yes, the fear of socialism, or to use a phrase that was thought to be a thing of the past — the Red Menace — is taken very seriously by Tea Party supporters. As it was in the 1950s, socialism (a kind of communism-lite) is something that many Americans love to hate." Froese goes on to state: "Libertarians hate the socialist because he or she threatens their liberty and takes their money through taxation. But there is a different and often overlooked reason why conservative Christians fear the socialist: Because the socialist is also an atheist."[422]

In conclusion, the moral issues facing the Tea Party are twofold. First, they are not recognising the fact that most people want the benefits of social services such as unemployment, disability and pension cheques – but just don't call it socialism. That's the domain for the left wing socialist Democrats. Second, although the people want the benefits, they don't want their taxes to pay for them. It can be easily said that the arguments of the Tea Party are high on emotion and rhetoric, and short on economic wisdom. Surely, the quality of life and the happiness experienced by the Scandinavian countries of Sweden, Norway, Finland and Denmark should be something that all American citizens should aspire to. This can only come from the morally responsible blend of fair taxation for all and a comprehensive range of social services. It means a more egalitarian society with a better distribution of wealth than what Americans currently enjoy. After all, isn't that what 92% of the population asked for?

David Dietz summed it up as follows;

"Constantly lowering taxes, slashing critical government programs, and catering to Wall Street by dismantling regulation is not the answer. It is part of the problem. It is no coincidence that the world's strongest and most stable economies (Germany, Scandinavia, Canada, Australia) all are able to mesh social welfare with an advantageous business climate.

"If America wants to regain its global edge and cement its economic dominance, the US must look to countries like Sweden, Norway, and others as a model of how the health of society is measured by the vivacity of the middle class. In doing so we must finally accept that taxes, regulations, and government programs do not necessarily impede economic growth, but can ensure it."[423]

These are wise words indeed; words that the Tea Party find difficult to understand. Perhaps this is why many consider that the Tea Party and morality are on the opposite sides of the fence.

Chapter 20

Donations, Lobbying and Political Corruption

∞∞∞∞

Donations to political candidates and parties have been commonplace since the US Constitution was written. After all, the lengthy United States electoral system is arguably the most cumbersome and most expensive in the developed world. As at 31st March 2012, donations to both political parties were in excess of $330 million.[424] However, this figure does not take into consideration the enormous dollar amount that American large corporates, with vested interests, pay for political advertising.

On 21st January 2010, The US Supreme Court held that the First Amendment prohibited the government from restricting independent political expenditures by corporations and unions.[425] In a 5-4 ruling, the court decision makes it legal for corporations, trade associations and non-profit organisations to use their treasury funds to pay for advertising that explicitly encourages the audience to vote, for or against, a particular candidate.

While this may be seen to be legal in the eyes of the politically biased Supreme Court (refer Chapter 24), it does raise many questions about the morality of such advertising. It is estimated that by the 6 Nov election, campaigns will have spent $2.6 billion, with 85% going to local TV.[426] In the same article, DiClemente estimated that CBS alone would receive around $230 million in political advertising.[427] On the surface, this may look as if it is just the way big corporations do business. It's all part of a normal day's work in corporate life.

When this is analysed more closely, one has to ask; what do these large corporates, trade associations etc. expect in return for their political support of a particular candidate? Surely, if their campaign is successful, then they would expect to receive political preference in the form of favourable legislation. Is this such a crime, in a democracy, one might ask? Unfortunately, it is, metaphorically speaking. In a democracy, people have voting rights and corporations and organisations do not, yet they often have a disproportionate amount of political clout, often to the detriment of the very citizens that voted for a particular party.

One case in point: The American Petroleum Institute (API), whose members include Exxon Mobil and Chevron, gave millions of dollars in political donations, mainly to the Republican Party in the 2010 elections.[428] According to the Centre for Responsive Politics, oil and gas companies gave about 77% of their political donations or $19.6 million to the Republican Party. (Oil and Gas were only the 15th largest source of political contributions leading up to the 2010 elections.)[429]

The reason for these one-sided contributions was to lobby against the repealing of $46 billion in subsidies and imposing pollution rules.[430] The API claims that greenhouse-gas regulations issued by the EPA are burdensome and a threat to the economic recovery. This in itself is an indictment on the oil industry; the same industry that lobbied Washington to exempt it from provisions in the major federal environmental statutes intended to protect human health and the environment. (Refer chapter 7.)

With corporate donations and the expectations of favours by Big Business, it comes as no surprise that the United States ranked a lowly 24th in a list of least corrupt countries in 2010.[431]

Watergate

The Watergate scandal of the 1970s has proven to everyone that corruption in politics comes from the very top. On 17th June 1972, five men broke into the Democratic National Committee Headquarters at the Watergate office complex in Washington, DC. The five men, who were arrested for breaking and entering, were found to be holding cash, which was later traced by the FBI to be connected to a slush fund belonging to the Committee for the Re-election of the President a fundraising group for the Nixon campaign.[432]

Further investigations proved that the Nixon Administration attempted in vain to cover-up its involvement with the scandal. The Watergate break-in eventually led to the arrest, trial and conviction of 43 people, including dozens of Nixon Administration staff members.[433]

President Nixon's downfall, which eventually led to his resigning the presidency on 9th August 1974,[434] came about from tape recordings he had in the Oval Office. These recordings proved beyond any doubt that the president was aware of what had taken place and had attempted to cover-up the break-in.[435] President Ford, who took over the presidency, pardoned Richard Nixon.

Chapter 21

Politics and Religion

∞∞∞∞

The United States Constitution calls for the separation between Church and State. But has this effectively happened? And is there a conflict between the professed ethics of the dominant Christian right and the policies of the Republican Party, to which they mostly support?

The first thing that an independent non-American observer sees is that wherever one looks, there is the expression "in God we trust." This is not too surprising, given that the United States has the largest Christian community in the world. Adopted as the official motto of the United States in 1956,[436] it has been on some US coins since 1864 and paper currency since 1957.[437] It is also the motto of the US State of Florida.

Regardless of one's religious beliefs, this clearly is a violation of the Establishment Clause of the First Amendment and the Separation of Church and State. It assumes a belief in a single transcendent deity. While this may be acceptable to adherents of the three Abrahamic religions, it may be offensive to the faiths of the nearly 4 billion people who have different beliefs. However, the motto has been challenged by 3 separate lawsuits, and has been found to be constitutional on each occasion.[438] Religious references are also embedded in the required singing of *The Star Spangled Banner* and *America*, in classrooms.[439]

Furthermore, the required recitation of the US Pledge of Allegiance was modified under an act of Congress to include the words, "under God".[440] Surely, this is a direct contravention of the very words in the US Constitution, which states;

> "No religious Test shall ever be required as a Qualification to any Office or public Trust under the United States."

Another example of how religion and politics are inseparable, every time the president, republican or democrat, addresses the nation or makes a political speech, it always ends with the words;

> "God bless you and may God bless the United States of America."

All these things may seem harmless enough on the surface, and as mentioned earlier, have been found to be acceptable by the courts, under the US Constitution. Yet, each time a reference to God is made in the classroom, in the oaths of office, in judiciary proceedings and in the president's speeches, it serves to indoctrinate the psyche of the American people that America has some sort of divine blessing and protection from God.

This is so engrained in the American belief system that it goes right to the very top. The belief that God is on our side has led to many immoral executive decisions. One such decision was when George W Bush launched an illegal attack on Iraq, without the approval of the United Nations, saying that he had discussed the matter with God and not Congress.[441] In a speech in Nashville in March 2008, Bush stated;

"that his policies in the region were predicated on the beliefs that freedom was a God-given right and "every human being bears the image of our maker."[442]

In another speech he made at the Opreyland Hotel, also in Nashville, he said;

"The liberty we value is not ours alone. Freedom is not America's gift to the world; it is God's gift to all humanity."

How many more people have to die in the name of God, before we finally understand that there is no room for religion in politics in *any* country? Separation of Church and State means exactly that. There are two points that clearly need to be made here. First, not too many would consider the United States to be a theocracy, as seen in countries such as Iran and Saudi Arabia. Second, no-one would want to discourage anyone from their own personal beliefs. That is not the point. But when the line between religion and politics becomes increasingly blurred, then in reality, the separation between Church and State becomes a very grey area.

Now we come to an area of discussion, which many might dispute, depending on their religious beliefs and their political leanings. According to one newspaper reporter, in the United States, religious adherents are more likely to vote Republican, while secularists have a tendency to vote Democrat.[443] This observation is supported by Notre Dame political scientist, David Campbell who claims;

"If I know whether you say grace before meals every day, I can probably predict how you vote,"

About 44 % of Americans say grace and most of them vote Republican.[444]

All this shows is that most people who are devout by nature will have a tendency to vote for the conservative side of politics. Fundamentally, there is no issue with this. People are in many ways tribal and will often follow the lead of their family, friends and their local congregation, regardless of their faith. This is healthy, living democracy at work. What is difficult to understand is how this can occur, when there is a clear mismatch of morality and ethics between the people and the political parties they support.

In many parts of America, as there is elsewhere, there are a growing number of citizens who are struggling to make ends meet. It's difficult enough for many families to find adequate shelter and food, without depending on the social consciousness of religious organisations. Medical and hospital expenses are beyond the reach of many. Fortunately, religions of all faiths are committed to helping the poor, the less fortunate and the needy. This is the real essence of religion; to ensure that everyone in the community has the basic essentials for survival available to them. This is largely due to the high moral values that most organised religions espouse. They are constantly raising money for these people and church volunteers are always available to lend a helping hand.

Politicians on the other hand, are not always in tune with the social consciousness of the churches. They are influenced by lobbyists, big business, army generals and the wealthy, all of whom have separate agendas; ones that do not take into consideration the views, wants or needs of society's poor and less fortunate. This is the nature of modern day western politics; one that's not just found in the United States alone. But there are differences between the two sides of politics, both liberal and conservative.

Voters who are more socially-minded are more likely to support liberal policies, which are aimed to favour the needy; policies such as health reform, unemployment benefits, pension plans and disability assistance. To accommodate these policies, the liberal side of politics looks to increase taxes, especially on the wealthy and increase government sponsored safety nets.

On the other hand, voters who have more conservative views prefer the status quo. They look to having reduced taxation and less government spending, particularly in the area of welfare. The reasons for this may stem from a legacy of the cold war and the remnants of McCarthyism. During the cold war, the then communist USSR was considered to be evil, socialist and atheistic. It was the antithesis of what Americans thought of themselves, namely righteous, free-enterprise capitalists and Christian. According to Pew Research, 60% of Americans still regard socialism as a dirty word, although this trend is gradually changing with the majority of 18-29 year olds in favour of it.[445] In the same poll, two other groups were positive about socialism; blacks and liberal democrats.

Many people believe that mainly white Christians, who live in the Southern and mid-western states, view socialism in a negative light. In many ways, they are caught in a time warp and the thought of any change to their way of life, even if it is for the betterment of their personal well-being, is treated with total distrust.

Yet in these very same states, is where we find the largest concentrations of fundamentalist Christians, most of whom will support the conservative side of politics. How they vote and who they support is not what is at issue here. What is intriguing is that these same people who no doubt abide by the moral and ethical principles of the Bible seem to support the party, which is least likely to abide by these very same principles. In fact, one of the main reasons that the Republican conservatives were so successful in the 2010 elections was because of the unqualified support of the Christian Right. There can be no doubt that a higher percentage of this demographic voted compared to the national average.

But the perceptions of the 60% of those who mistrust socialism are largely misguided, partly because of culture and partly because of media bias. Today, when we mention socialism, we think of countries in Northern Europe. In these countries, they have a high degree of education, relatively no poverty and are amongst the most contented people in the world. In fact, the 4 Northern European countries of, Norway, Denmark, Sweden and Finland ranked 1, 2, 5, and 7 respectively, in a recent analysis, determining the world's happiest countries.[446] The United States could only manage 10th. In English speaking countries, Australia, 3rd, New Zealand, 4th and Canada 6th all ranked higher than the United States. All of these countries have managed to balance taxation, government size and social policies, without the sky falling.

In summary, the concept of socialism, which is looking after the less fortunate in the world, is in many ways, what religious philosophy is all about. Yet the same people, who abide by this philosophy, find it totally abhorrent when it comes to politics. If Americans really want more equality in income and lifestyle, less homelessness, less poverty and a decreased gap between the rich and the poor, then perhaps they need only to turn to their own religious beliefs for the answers. Socialism is not communism and its success in Northern Europe proves that it can work. Yes, it means higher taxes for the wealthy and more government controlled social services, but it could result in Americans being a happier country. It would also stop the less fortunate from being marginalised in a society, where there are no excuses for allowing this to occur. While there is no room for religion in politics, there is ample room for individuals to use their religious moral ethics to convince politicians that the time for progressive change is long overdue.

Chapter 22

The CIA, Ethics and Morality

∞∞∞∞

The Genesis of the CIA

The CIA was created by Congress and signed into law by President Harry S Truman in 1947. Its predecessor was the Office of Strategic Services (OSS) during World War II. In its early years, the CIA conducted a number of covert operations, which many still consider to be highly immoral, if not technically illegal under US law.

Examples of CIA involvement in international affairs include; the overthrow of a democratically elected government during the 1953 Iranian coup d'état, attempt to assassinate Fidel Castro, after the overthrow of the Batista government in Cuba and the failed Bay of Pigs invasion in April 1961.[447]

Then there was the infamous incident when Gary Powers was shot down flying a U-2 over Russia on a reconnaissance mission in 1960. At first, the United States claimed that Powers had strayed off course during a weather observation mission.[448]

However, as the plane landed almost intact, the Russians didn't accept this version of events. After intense interrogation by the KGB over several months, Powers finally confessed and apologised for his role in espionage.[449]

Then in 1974, investigative reporter, Seymour Hersh broke the news about the CIAs "Family Jewels" in the New York Times claiming that the CIA had been involved in assassination attempts and illegally spying on some 7,000 US anti-war activists.[450]

Ethics According to the CIA

There will always be questions raised when societies with supposed high ethical values, can sanctify the use of violence on citizens of other sovereign nations, friendly or hostile, or restrict their own personal liberties on security grounds. The war on terrorism has brought many of these questions to the fore in American society.

How can the CIA justify its actions when clearly they violate the very moral ethic that it is designed to protect, as spelled out in the American Constitution? Why is this double standard (some would say hypocrisy) condoned by the American government and to some extent, the American public? In order to get a clearer understanding on how these social conflicts can be justified, we need only look to what the CIA says in regards to these issues. According to the CIA, its core values are:

- **Service -** We put country first and Agency before self. Quiet patriotism is our hallmark. We are dedicated to the mission, and we pride ourselves on our extraordinary responsiveness to the needs of our customers.

- **Integrity** - We uphold the highest standards of conduct. We seek and speak the truth - to our colleagues and to our customers. We honour those Agency officers who have come before us and we honour the colleagues with whom we work today.
- **Excellence** - We hold ourselves - and each other - to the highest standards. We embrace personal accountability. We reflect on our performance and learn from that reflection.[451]

But a former CIA agent, John Stockwell tells quite a different story. In a lecture entitled "The Secret Wars of the CIA", he makes the following statement;

"The CIA has been called into question on several occasions for some of the tactics it employs to carry out its missions. At times these tactics have included torture, funding and training of groups and organizations that would later participate in killing of civilians and other non-combatants and would try or succeed in overthrowing democratically elected governments, human experimentation, and targeted killings and assassinations."[452]

Clearly, when it comes to ethics and morality, what happens in realty within the CIA is considerably remote from the rhetoric it promotes. So let's take a look at some specific examples, where American ethical, legal and Constitutional values have been compromised by the CIA. While each of these events could be "justified" as being part of the war on terrorism, there are still many unanswered questions which need to be addressed.

Capture of Osama bin Ladin

The 2nd May 2011 was a significant day in the fight against al Qaeda and international terrorism. After Osama bin Ladin was killed on that day, most people in the western world would have felt a little easier about their future. Some would say that the killing of bin Ladin was a just result, given his role in past terrorist activities, in particular, the devastating attacks of 911.

Nevertheless, the way in which he was tracked and finally killed raises a number of serious questions about the actions of the CIA in locating him, and the American government in choosing to have him assassinated on foreign soil. To recap, the CIA recruited a Pakistani doctor, Dr Shakil Afridi, to work undercover to collect blood samples that could identify bin Ladin's family.[453]

Although it may seem to have been clever at first glance, the fallout from their actions could have serious long-term effects on people's health in the parts of the world where they are most vulnerable. The problem is that many people may die as a result of this action, because they may be suspicious that any vaccination program might be a CIA plot.

Samuel Worthington, the president of an alliance of some 200 NGOs that operate abroad, summed it up this way;[454]

"Since reports of the CIA campaign first surfaced last summer, we have seen a continued erosion of US NGOs' ability to deliver critical humanitarian programs in Pakistan as well as an uptick in targeted violence against humanitarian workers. I fear the CIA's activities in Pakistan and the perception that US NGOs have ties with intelligence efforts may have contributed to these alarming developments."

One immediate casualty of the CIAs action was that Dr Afridi was sentenced by a Pakistani court to 33 years imprisonment for treason.[455]

There is one other question that is troublesome from a purely ethical point of view. Did the United States have the right to assassinate bin Ladin, or should he have been captured for trial on the basis of being innocent until proven guilty? Perhaps it's best to leave this question to the citizens of the United States to decide.

Use of Drones

The ever-increasing use of drones in foreign countries, such as Afghanistan, Pakistan, Somalia and Yemen is causing many in the public to question their legitimacy. According to one report, the use of drones has killed up to 830 civilians, including many women and children, might have been killed by drone attacks in Pakistan, 138 in Yemen and 57 in Somalia. Hundreds more have been injured.[456] These facts alone should be enough to have the use of drones banned from use in international sovereign nations, except in self-defence. Unfortunately, the US government appears to be in complete denial on this issue. Whitehouse counter-terrorism advisor, John Brennan, acknowledged that there may be civilian deaths from drone attacks, but these are "exceedingly rare".[457]

The use of drones has increased significantly under the Obama Administration. According to Robert Grenier, who headed the CIAs counter-terrorism centre from 2004-2006, there have been at least 275 drone attacks in Pakistan alone.[458] A recent report stated that a drone accidently hit a mosque, where a funeral was being held for a Pakistani militant, killed on the previous day by a drone attack. This action prompted a further comment from Grenier who said;

> "We have gone a long way down the road of creating a situation where we are creating more enemies than we are removing from the battlefield. We are already there with regards to Pakistan and Afghanistan."[459]

The Bureau of Investigative Journalism (BIJ) claims that there have been 41 confirmed drone strikes in Yemen and up to 55 unconfirmed strikes. Grenier believes that these strikes will lend further support to Islamists and further anti-US sentiment. As the Yemeni people have large families and are very tribal, the degree of hatred against the United States could escalate and boil over to other Islamists communities in neighbouring countries. In the end, the use of drones to flush out "suspected" enemies of the state could well and truly be counter-productive.

Peace in the world is possible but remains delicately poised. The last thing that America and the world needs is another clash of civilisations as witnessed during the Holy Wars of the dark ages.

When Assassination Becomes "Targeted Killing"

Targeted killing is when a government or its agents deliberately target a civilian, who is not in the government's custody. The target is usually a person, who allegedly takes part in armed conflict or terrorism.[460] According to Georgetown Law Professor, Gary Solis, this is perfectly legitimate because alleged terrorists are targeted in self-defence. While this makes it a killing, it is not a crime. On the other hand, an assassination is murder and therefore is considered to be a crime.[461]

However, the American Civil Liberties Union takes an opposing view. In its website, it states;

> "A program of targeted killing far from any battlefield, without charge or trial, violates the constitutional guarantee of due process. It also violates international law, under which lethal force may be used outside armed conflict zones only as a last resort to prevent imminent threats, when non-lethal means are not available. Targeting people who are suspected of terrorism for execution, far from any war zone, turns the whole world into a battlefield."[462]

Whichever side of the argument that people wish to accept, the fact remains that targeted killing, like assassinations are highly immoral. There may be legal loopholes, which are used to defend the actions of the CIA and there may even be emotional arguments causing citizens to accept these killings. But in the end, they should turn to their own moral values and spiritual beliefs, in order to find answers to this strange interpretation of what is nothing short of murder.

Chapter 23

The Patriot Act

∞∞∞

Afer the devastating attacks on the United States on 911, the government had to be seen to be taking quick and drastic action that would minimise the chances of these types of attacks from ever occurring again. One of the more controversial responses was the introduction of the USA Patriot Act in October 2001. The Act is an acronym for "Uniting and Strengthening America by Providing Appropriate Tools Required to Intercept and Obstruct Terrorism".[463]

According to author, Grayden Carter, the Patriot Act, which was passed without debate or any public hearings, is a clear violation of the First, Fourth, Fifth, Sixth, Eighth and Fourteenth amendments to the US Constitution.[464] One of the major criticisms of the Act came from the American Civil Liberties Union (ACLU). Their initial response was scathing, not only to the expediency of the Act (just 45 days after 911) but also on the loss of American civil liberties; something that most Americans felt protected from in the US Constitution. In particular, the ACLU criticised the unchecked power that the Act gave to access personal records of individuals, including;

financial records, medical histories, Internet usage, bookstore purchases, library usage, travel patterns, or any other activity that leaves a record.[465] According to the ACLU, the Patriot Act means:

- The government no longer has to show evidence that the subjects of search orders are an "agent of a foreign power," a requirement that previously protected Americans against abuse of this authority.
- The FBI does not even have to show a reasonable suspicion that the records are related to criminal activity, much less the requirement for "probable cause" that is listed in the Fourth Amendment to the Constitution. All the government needs to do is make the broad assertion that the request is related to an ongoing terrorism or foreign intelligence investigation.
- Judicial oversight of these new powers is essentially non-existent. The government must only certify to a judge - with no need for evidence or proof - that such a search meets the statute's broad criteria, and the judge does not even have the authority to reject the application.
- Surveillance orders can be based in part on a person's First Amendment activities, such as the books they read, the Web sites they visit, or a letter to the editor they have written.
- A person or organization forced to turn over records is prohibited from disclosing the search to anyone. As a result of this gag order, the subjects of surveillance

never even find out that their personal records have been examined by the government. That undercuts an important check and balance on this power: the ability of individuals to challenge illegitimate searches.[466]

Further concerns about the Act came from the Electronic Frontier Foundation;[467] the Constitutional Rights Foundation;[468] the American Library Association[469] and many others. But perhaps the most damning criticisms came from a number of states, cities and towns. According the Bill of Rights Defence Committee, three states (Alaska, Hawaii and Vermont), and 149 cities, towns and counties have passed resolutions protesting some provisions of the Patriot Act.[470]

Interestingly, the much loved and often quoted, Abraham Lincoln in a rather prophetic statement said;

"Those who sacrifice freedom for security deserve neither."[471]

But is it possible that the American public have become blasé about the Patriot Act? In a petition to the Obama Administration in Sept 2011, some 22,703 signatories asked for the Patriot Act to be repealed. Given the total population of the United States, this is a rather small number.[472] Perhaps the effect of the global financial crisis has replaced this piece of legislation on the nation's media headlines, causing it to go onto the back burner.

The fact that the USA Patriot Act was rushed into legislation and violated the basic rights of American citizens, who thought they were protected by the Constitution, is not the only adverse aspect of the Act. What people may not be aware of is that the Act may have prevented food aid to get to starving men, women and children in Somalia. Speaking at a seminar in Helsinki in April, 2012, Ken Menkhaus, professor of Political Science at Davidson College in North Carolina, claimed that humanitarian organisations suspended food aid to drought-stricken areas controlled by al-Shabaab, for fear of violating the USA Patriot Act.[473] Professor Menkhaus said;

> "There are plenty of western countries, including my own government, who would like to see the conversation stop right there and say it was all Al-Shabaab's fault." However, the other bottleneck was US policy, which "de facto criminalises any transactions in southern Somali."[474]

The once moral outrage that was directed at President Bush on the issue of the Patriot Act has almost become completely silent. So much so that when President Obama signed a renewal of the Patriot Act, while he was in the UK, in May 2011, there was hardly a whisper from the liberal side of politics.[475] When it comes to ethics, sometimes even the general public are quick to forget.

Chapter 24

The Judicial System

∞∞∞∞

In most western societies, the judicial system is deemed to be separate and independent from the legislature. In the case of the United States, it is the US Constitution, which sets the ground rules for the selection of the judiciary. However, appointment of federal judges has become extremely politicised under this process. This is certainly the case with the selection of Justices to the Supreme Court, as indicated in Fig 24.1.[476]

Fig 24.1 (Selection of Supreme Court Justices)

Year	Appointed by Republicans	Appointed By Democrats
Current	5	4
2008	7	2
2004	7	2
2000	7	2
1996	7	2
1992	8	1

1988	7	2
1984	7	2
1980	7	2
1976	7	2
1972	6	3
1968	4	5
1964	4	5
1960	5	4

As you can see from the above list, Justices chosen by Republican presidents held a majority for 44 out of the last 52 years. Yet the Republicans were in power for only 28 out of the last 52 years. The reason for this discrepancy is that Supreme Court Justices are appointed for life and a new president of either persuasion may not get the opportunity of making a new appointment.

Unfortunately, this system allows for politically motivated decisions which, to many in the outside world, is nothing short of political corruption. Perhaps one of the most controversial decisions was the one taken after the 2000 presidential elections. In a 5-4 majority decision, the Supreme Court effectively handed George W Bush the presidency. It was not to anyone's surprise that the five Justices, who voted for Bush, were all appointed by Republican presidents.

In another issue that is of concern to many Americans, is the number of innocent people in American jails, many of whom are on death row. To date, DNA has exonerated in excess of 270 people for crimes they did not commit. While this seems like a large number, it is only a very small percentage of the 2 million men and women, who are currently incarcerated in

American prisons.[477] It just proves that occasionally courts and jurors will get the verdict wrong. This is only natural, particularly when many of the facts are circumstantial. But how many innocent people on death row have to die, before the death sentence is finally abolished?

One further area of concern with the American judicial system is just how unreasonable some of the fines and compensation decisions can be, particularly on individuals. One such case, which was heard in 2009, was the case against a Boston University student for downloading just 30 songs from a file sharing site. Joel Tenenbaum, 28 was fined a ridiculous $675,000 for the offence. Although this was appealed and the fine subsequently reduced to $67,500, the 1st US Circuit Court of Appeals re-instated it.[478]

Given the tens of millions of Americans, who have used these sites in the past, it is an indictment on the American justice system that Tenenbaum has been singled out to shoulder the burden of all the others. After all, before the Internet, Tenenbaum could have easily gone to a friend's house and recorded the same 30 songs onto a tape or CD. That was perfectly acceptable. The only thing that has changed is that he does not know from whom he is copying the songs. While the recording industry may have some legitimate claims to lost income as a result of these file-sharing sites, suing an individual for that amount is obscene to say the least. It shows the immense lobbying and litigation power of the recording industry. Unfortunately in this instance, the courts, in siding with big business have got it wrong. In centuries past, a man would be sent to prison for stealing a loaf of bread. Most of us thought that we were over these harsh penalties for such trivial crimes. Obviously we are not.

In this case, Tenenbaum's lawyers estimated that the average teenager downloads about 800 songs,[479] so why was this University student singled out for downloading just 30? If there was ever a case to be answered, surely it should have been with the file sharing websites and not the people who used it. Perhaps there may have been a different outcome if during the jury selection process in the original trial, they were asked just two questions; have you ever downloaded a song or music video from a file sharing site, without sending money to the publisher? Or, have you ever borrowed a CD or a book from someone you know, without sending money to the publisher? I would suggest that if these questions were asked, the lawyers would *still* be trying to find 12 jurors. The result can only be described as a total indictment on the judicial system; one that has the stench of political corruption at the highest levels.

Campaign Financing Ruling

The United States promotes itself as a democracy, upon which all other democracies should be based. They are free to assemble, enjoy free speech and everyone has a right to vote. However, one of the pillars of American democracy, the judicial system, is often seen to be too closely aligned with the conservative side of politics, as indicated previously.

One such example was the 5-4 decision in January 2010, which removed limits on corporate campaign spending. The decision in the *Citizens United* case effectively allows corporations to spend unlimited amounts of money to elect or defeat candidates; a decision slammed by the Democrats and many lawmakers.

One serious objector was James Raskin, Professor of Constitutional Law at American University and a Maryland State Senator. His outspoken opinion may not be liked by the conservative side of politics, but his statement has a refreshing honesty that is hard to argue against. It confirms the fact that the US judicial system is inherently flawed in its structure. Raskin said;

"With its 2010 decision in Citizens United, the Roberts-led Court essentially cemented the institution's return to a class-bound right-wing judicial activism. Just as the Supreme Court went to war against social reform and President Franklin Delano Roosevelt's New Deal in the 1930s, just as it nullified the meaning of Equal Protection in sanctifying "separate but equal" in Plessy v. Ferguson in 1896, just as it expressed the Supreme Court's pro-slavery and racist jurisprudence in the Dred Scott decision in 1857, the Citizens United decision secured the contemporary Court's unfolding legacy as the unabashed champion of corporate power and class privilege."[480]

When it comes to issues of national importance, it is absolutely clear that the US Supreme Court is politically and ideological aligned to the two major political parties. Unfortunately for social justice, in the last half century, it appears that the Supreme Court has done the bidding of the Republican Party on behalf of large corporates and the wealthy and influential 1%.

This fact did not escape the attention of President Obama, who responded after the Court decision by stating;

"With its ruling today, the Supreme Court has given a green light to a new stampede of special interest money in our politics...a major victory for Big Oil, Wall Street banks, health insurance companies and the other powerful interests that marshal their power every day in Washington to drown out the voices of everyday Americans."[481]

Perhaps it was US Rep Christopher Van Hollen Jr. (D-Dist. 8) of Kensington who summed the feelings amongst ethical seeking Americans. Van Hollen criticized the ruling during a press conference, calling Thursday...

"...a very, very sad day for American democracy." He added, "It will allow the biggest corporations of the United States to engage in the buying and selling of elections."

The real challenge for US democracy is not freedom of the press or freedom of speech, or any other factors that make Western democracy what it is. The challenge is to change the Constitution to allow for a different method of selection for the Supreme Court Justices that is independent from political influences. Unfortunately, this is not likely to happen and the injustices of the judicial system are set to continue for the foreseeable future. It is another example in the conflict between what is morally right and what is politically expedient.

However, if we allowed ourselves to fantasise for a moment, here is a Supreme Court selection criteria that just might work;

1) Start with a clean sheet and allow both the Democrats and the Republicans to select 4 Justices each
2) The 9th Justice to be selected by the American Bar Association from a pool of 4-5 (or more) from the circuit court of appeals judges, with a different one chosen at random for each case.
3) The 8 permanent Justices would be required to retire at 70. They would then be replaced by the same party that selected them.
4) The pool of 4-5 Justices would also be required to retire at 70 and be replaced by the ABA.

This suggestion may not be perfect, but it is a far sight better than the politically biased one that is available today.

Footnote: On 28th June 2012, the Supreme Court went against their policy of politically motivated decisions by claiming the Obama Care health plan to be legally constitutional. The 5-4 decision was a welcome relief to the 30 million Americans, who would now have health insurance for the first time. Needless to say, the decision was a great disappointment to Republicans, who fought unsuccessfully to have the legislation overturned.

Chapter 25

Moral Questions
Of the
Bush Administration

∞∞∞∞

L ooking back at George W Bush's term in office, there is
one word that is frequently used to describe his presidency,
and that word is incompetent. Sure, he had a series of events
that made his term difficult; events such as 911, Hurricane
Katrina and the global financial crisis. This is not surprising,
given a CNN poll on 21st October 2008 that showed an
approval rating of only 27%.[482] His incompetency is best
summed up by Julian Zelizer, professor of history and public
affairs at Princeton University's Woodrow Wilson School, who
said;

"He is seen as incompetent in terms of how he handled domestic and foreign policy. He is seen as pushing for an agenda to the right of the nation and doing so through executive power that ignored the popular will."[483]

Whether or not historians will judge him as incompetent in the future is yet to be determined. But his incompetency is not the main focus of this book. While there may be certain unavoidable situations, which occur on a president's watch that may render him incompetent in the eyes of many, there is no excuse for making decisions, which are immoral, and possibly even illegal, in nature.

There have been many articles and books written about George W Bush and how many of the decisions that were made by him that were considered to be highly immoral. One such book is entitled *What We've Lost* by Grayden Carter and it makes for extremely enlightening reading. At the time of writing, Grayden Carter had been editor-in-chief of Vanity Fair since 1992.

So just how does George W Bush rate in terms of morality? We have already mentioned several instances in this book and now, with the help of Grayden Carter's book, it's time to recap and make an honest assessment of Bush's presidency.

- Illegal invasion of Afghanistan, in an effort to find and kill one man, Osama bin Ladin, where between 17,000 and 37,000 civilians, nearly 3,000 coalition casualties at a cost of $468 billion (refer chapter 18) – morality test -
FAILED

- Illegal invasion of Iraq, based on trumped up charges of weapons of mass destruction and the obsession to eliminate Saddam Hussein. The cost – 100,000 civilian deaths, 4,500 American casualties at a cost of nearly $3 trillion (refer chapter 18) - morality test - FAILED

- Illegal rendition and torture (refer chapter 18) – morality test - FAILED

- Illegal assassinations, also known as targeted killing (refer chapter 22) – morality test - FAILED

- Illegal detention of suspected terrorists at Guantanamo without trial or legal representation – morality test - FAILED

- Unashamed military and political support for Israel, while they continue to encroach on into Palestinian Territory with new housing developments, whilst giving nothing to help the Palestinians (refer chapter 17) – morality test - FAILED

- Lowering taxes on the wealthy – morality test FAILED

- Introduction of the Patriot ACT, which violated several amendments to the US Constitution (refer chapter 23) -morality test - FAILED

- Allowing Big Oil to drill for gas and oil using hydraulic fracturing techniques and allowing them to ignore several environmental acts including the Clean Water Act (refer chapter 7) – morality test - FAILED

- The introduction of changes to the Medicare Bill in November 2003, which favoured the already profitable Pharmaceutical Industry, but did little for the people who could afford it the least, e.g. middle income pensioner out-of-pocket drug costs soared by over 60%.[484] Then there was the disgraceful way in which the Bill was passed through the House[485] - morality test - FAILED

- Complicit in stacking the circuit courts of appeals with conservative right-leaning views, ensuring that Republican ideology will be entrenched for decades to come. While this may seem to be politically advantageous, it certainly is an indictment on the whole selection process for circuit court of appeals and Supreme Court judges. Stacking the courts

effectively disenfranchises 50% of US citizens–
morality test -
FAILED

- Supposedly advocated the "free market" in public,
while at the same time increasing farm subsidies to
$180 billion over 10 years, an increase of 70%[486] -
morality test -
FAILED

President Bush was elected to serve the people of the United
States. As president, he was required to be on call 24 hours a
day, 7 days a week. But even presidents need holiday time to
recharge the batteries from what is a very demanding job. But
did President Bush fail the people in this regard, as well?
Records show that he spent 40% of his time at 3 holiday
retreats, while he was in office.[487] We'll let the reader be the
judge of that question.

There is much more that can be written on this subject, as
Grayden Carter has done in *What We've Lost*. To continue on
will be just repeating what has already been written elsewhere.
Suffice to say that President Bush will not only be remembered
as the most incompetent president in history, he might also be
remembered as the president who decided, that if there was a
conflict between political ideological power and the moral well-
being of Americans, he chose ideology and power on almost
every occasion.

America's Lost Morality

Part V

The Final Chapter

America's Lost Morality

Chapter 26

Is America's Morality Lost Forever?

∞∞∞∞

I remember my childhood days, growing up in Canada and living in awe of everything American. The movies said it all; how America won the war and how the west was won. They led the world with great new technology such as the advent of television, washing machines and refrigerators. It was a time when children played innocently in the streets after school and on the weekends and we never had to lock the door, if we were just going out to do some shopping. It was a great time to be alive, when we could walk to school each morning, sometimes through 60cm (2 feet) of freshly fallen snow. We had lots of fun and we looked forward to the evening family meal, when we all sat around the table and talked about everything and sometimes about nothing in particular. Those were great days that many of us, that are now of the older generation fondly remember.

But life, values and ethics have changed dramatically since the '50s. It is a different world today; a world filled with violence, terrorism, uncertainty and fear. People no longer want to walk the streets alone at night. The war against drugs has failed and crime rates have dramatically increased. We have become obsessed with the rich and famous and try to emulate them by wearing designer clothes and living in ever-larger homes. We drive bigger and faster cars and live ever more stressful lives; a slave to our computers, mobile phones and social networking sites.

Travelling anywhere in the world is a tortuous experience as we stand in ever-increasing queues at the airport while our luggage and bodies are scanned for illicit drugs, weapons or bombs. Planes are getting larger but the seating in economy class is getting smaller. Services in the airline industry are a shadow of what they were even 30 years ago.

Since the '50s we have been bombarded with advertising on fast food, where the bottom line is that the *quantity* of food we eat is better for us than the *quality* – as long as it's cheap and contains copious amounts of salt, sugar and saturated fats. Our waistlines have expanded as a result, with 36% of American adults and 17% of children are considered to be obese according to the CDC in 2010.[488]

Yes, there have been many changes in lifestyle since the end of World War II. Change is inevitable and in many aspects there have been many positive changes; changes such as immunisation from disease, lifestyle products that make our lives a little easier and enormous advances in technology. But are all these things worth what we have lost along the way?

Our desire for big cars, SUVs, neon lights and air conditioning may be promoted as great lifestyle choices that we now enjoy, but at what cost? The United States, with only 5% of the world's population produces nearly 25% of the world's greenhouse gases.[489] Only China produces more greenhouse gases than the United States, but China has 4 times the population. And we call this progress?

As we have seen, the gap between rich and poor is widening in the United States. Governments of both persuasions have been seduced and even controlled by some degree by big multinational corporations and their lobbyists. In each passing decade, the will of the people has counted for less, as they continue to be indoctrinated by slick media ads and biased political reporting from certain media networks. It comes as no surprise that the top 1% of income earners are the ones who are in control. Unfortunately, their relentless quest for power has infected many Western countries as we see sportspeople, actors, radio and television personalities and executive salaries skyrocket, even in the face of adversity as caused by the Global Financial Crisis.

The essence of the true democratic model has failed us and there are few signs that this is about to change. The American people weren't listened to when Bush went to war in Iraq. They weren't listened to when they expressed their concerns about climate change, and they are not being listened to when they complain about the discrepancy between the rich and the poor.

In the last 60 years, we have seen America's reputation change from a country to be admired to a country that is almost universally despised, except by a handful of mainly English-speaking and European nations. There are a number of reasons for this, many of which are discussed in the book, *Why do People Hate America?* by Ziauddin Sardar and Maerryl Wyn Davies. The question we have tried to answer is what role the decline in moral values at a political and business level has played in this outcome?

Let us summarise some of the major changes in the political landscape over the last 60 years, which have led to this decline. President Eisenhower warned of "the acquisition of unwarranted influence, whether sought or unsought, by the military-industrial complex."[490] How prophetic this statement was. It's almost as if that there is a belief in the upper echelons of American politics that the only way to stay ahead of the rest of the world, is to continue to exercise its military might as a means of misguidedly trying to influence the rest of the world that there is only one right way – the American way. It is the classic "might is right" principle that has been part of dominant empires of the past.

Between the attack on Pearl Harbor and 911, 2001, the United States has been involved in no less than 200 military incursions in wars against communism, terrorism, drugs or anything else that the United States deemed to be against the American way.[491] And that figure does not include the illegal intrusions into Afghanistan and Iraq. Also, in his essay entitled *PERPETUAL WAR FOR PERPETUAL PEACE: How We Got to Be So Hated,* Gore Vidal claims that in most instances, the United States struck the first blow.[492]

These countless and mostly unjustifiable military actions kept the ever-powerful arms manufacturing industry in business, allowing them to make huge profits, some of which was re-directed back into election campaigns. It was a cosy arrangement. You keep us in business and we will keep you in power. It may come as little surprise to know that in the year 2000, the United States, with 5% of the world's population, had a military budget that was as big as the total of all of the other 190 countries combined.[493]

Add to this the extravagance of Wall Street executives to defraud the American public and plunge the world into a global recession and you have the perfect storm. The challenges of food, water and natural resource shortages took a back seat. So did the challenge of global warming and a deteriorating environment. Most importantly, the might of the triad of business, military and government, backed by the political stacking of the courts has left many Americans in poverty and without hope. This period in history will be remembered as an immoral injustice against the middle class and a travesty against democracy. I can say with some certainty that this is not the America that the founding fathers would have envisaged.

The final questions that remain are, has the United States gone past the tipping point; a point of no return? Can the government learn from its mistakes and make a paradigm shift in thinking, so that a true ethical democracy can be returned to the people? Will the United States ever be able to revert back to a time when violence was minimised; divorces were rare; consumerism was not excessive; when companies cared more about their employees and customers than they did about their share price; when the aspiration to a successful and happy middle-class life was attainable through hard-work and company loyalty; and when morality was not only a way of life,

221

but also an expectation from governments, business and the judiciary?

It seems that in many ways America has lost its way since the end of World War II. The reason for the decline in morality can best be summed up by three philosophies, the themes of which have been discussed in some detail in this book. These philosophies are; "greed is good", "might is right" and "God is on my side." For positive changes in moral values to occur, the people of this once great nation need to seriously question these philosophies and how they affect the world we all must live in. Whether there is sufficient collective desire to effect the changes necessary to return the United States to its formal glory, only time will tell.

Appendix A

List of countries with firearm-related deaths

Country	Total firearm-related death rate	Homicides	Suicides	Unintentional deaths
South Africa	74.57	74.57	NA	NA
Colombia	51.77	51.77	NA	NA
El Salvador	50.36	50.36	NA	NA
Jamaica	47.44	47.44	NA	NA
Honduras	46.70	46.70	NA	NA
Guatemala	38.52	38.52	NA	NA
Swaziland	37.16	37.16	NA	NA
Thailand	33.00	33.00	NA	NA
Brazil	14.15	10.58	0.73	0.28
Estonia	12.74	8.07	3.13	0.93
Panama	12.92	12.92	NA	NA
Mexico	12.07	9.88	0.91	1.27
United States	10.27	4.14	5.71	0.23
Philippines	9.46	9.46	NA	NA
Argentina	9.19	2.11	3.05	0.32
Paraguay	7.35	7.35	NA	NA
Nicaragua	7.14	7.14	NA	NA
Finland	6.86	0.86	5.78	0.12
Northern Ireland	6.82	5.24	1.34	0.12
Switzerland	6.4	0.58	5.61	0.13
France	6.35	0.44	5.14	0.11
Canada	4.78	0.76	3.72	0.22
Zimbabwe	4.75	4.75	NA	NA
Austria	4.56	0.42	4.06	0.05
Norway	4.39	0.3	3.95	0.12
Portugal	3.72	1.28	1.28	0.21
Belgium	3.48	0.6	2.56	0.06
Costa Rica	3.32	3.32	NA	NA

America's Lost Morality

Uruguay	3.24	3.24	NA	NA
Slovenia	3.07	0.35	2.51	0.2
Barbados	3	3	NA	NA
Israel	3	0.72	1.84	0.13
Italy	2.95	1.66	1.11	0.11
Australia	2.94	0.44	2.35	0.11
New Zealand	2.66	0.17	2.14	0.09
Denmark	2.6	0.23	2.25	0.04
Sweden	2.36	0.18	2.09	0.03
Slovakia	2.17	2.17	NA	NA
Peru	1.87	1.87	NA	NA
Czech Republic	1.77	1.77	NA	NA
Germany	1.57	0.22	1.17	0.04
Greece	1.5	0.59	0.84	0.04
Azerbaijan	1.47	1.47	NA	NA
Macedonia	1.28	1.28	NA	NA
Kuwait	1.25	0.36	0.06	0
Hungary	1.21	0.23	0.88	0.09
Ireland	1.21	0.03	0.94	0.11
Latvia	1.2	1.2	NA	NA
India	0.93	0.93	NA	NA
Spain	0.9	0.21	0.43	0.25
Bulgaria	0.77	0.77	NA	NA
Netherlands	0.7	0.36	0.31	0.01
Scotland	0.58	0.19	0.33	0.02
Moldova	0.47	0.47	NA	NA
Lithuania	0.46	0.46	NA	NA
Taiwan	0.42	0.15	0.12	0.11
Belarus	0.38	0.38	NA	NA
Ukraine	0.35	0.35	NA	NA
Poland	0.29	0.29	NA	NA
England/ Wales	0.46	0.07	0.33	0.01
Singapore	0.24	0.07	0.17	0
Hong Kong	0.19	0.12	0.07	0
Mauritius	0.19	0	0.09	0.09
Qatar	0.18	0.18	NA	NA
South Korea	0.13	0.04	0.02	0.05
Japan	0.07	0.02	0.04	0
Chile	0.06	0.06	NA	NA

Appendix B

Oil Reserves and Annual Usage

Year	Annual Usage Billion Barrels p/a (2% increase p/a)	Accumulated Total Usage	World Supply (Billion Barrels)
2001	27.5	27.5	
2002	28.1	55.6	
2003	28.6	84.2	
2004	29.2	113.3	
2005	29.8	143.1	1292.6
2006	30.4	173.5	1262.2
2007	31.0	204.4	1231.3
2008	31.6	236.0	1199.7
2009	32.2	268.3	1167.5
2010	32.9	301.1	1134.6
2011	33.5	334.6	1101.1
2012	34.2	368.8	1066.9
2013	34.9	403.7	1032.0
2014	35.6	439.3	996.4
2015	36.3	475.6	960.1
2016	37.0	512.6	923.1
2018	37.8	550.3	885.4
2019	38.5	588.8	846.9
2020	39.3	628.1	807.6
2021	40.1	668.2	767.5

2022	40.9	709.0	726.7
2023	41.7	750.7	685.0
2024	42.5	793.2	642.5
2025	43.4	836.6	599.1
2026	44.2	880.8	554.9
2027	45.1	925.9	509.8
2028	46.0	972.0	463.7
2029	46.9	1018.9	416.8
2030	47.9	1066.8	368.9
2031	48.8	1115.6	320.1
2032	49.8	1165.4	270.3
2033	50.8	1216.2	219.5
2034	51.8	1268.1	167.6
2035	52.9	1320.9	114.8
2036	53.9	1374.8	60.9
2037	55.0	1429.8	5.9

Notes

[1] Wikipedia.org/wiki/Secular_ethics
[2] US Religious Landscape Survey
[3] Religious Tolerance website – www.religioustolerance.org
[4] BBC News. April 3, 2007
[5] National Church Life Survey, Media release, February 28, 2004
[6] Anna Gandziarowski, The Puritan Legacy to American Politics (2010) p. 2
[7] John Winthrop – A Model of Christian Charity -163
[8] American Spectator – March 2011
[9] http://edition.cnn.com/2012/04/02/us/california-shooting/index.html?hpt=hp_t1
[10] http://www.smallarmssurvey.org/fileadmin/docs/A-Yearbook/2007/en/Small-Arms-Survey-2007-Chapter-02-annexe-4-EN.pdf
[11] http://www.wect.com/story/17270330/lead-instigator-wanted-to-press-charges-in-trayvon-case
[12] http://abcnews.go.com/m/story?id=16011674
[13] www.theage.com.au – 20 May 2012
[14] Ibid
[15] Nick O'Malley, US Correspondent with Washington Post
[16] CBS Miami, 20 March 2012
[17] http://www.smh.com.au
[18] ABC Foreign Correspondent – Michael Brissenden March 2011
[19] Nat'l Ctr. for Injury Prevention & Control, US Centers for Disease Control and Prevention, Web-based Injury Statistics Query & Reporting System (WISQARS) Injury Mortality Reports, 1999-2009, for National, Regional, and States (Sept. 2011)
[20] http://en.wikipedia.org/wiki/List_of_countries_by_firearm-related_death_rate
[21] http://www.smallarmssurvey.org/fileadmin/docs/A-Yearbook/2007/en/Small-Arms-Survey-2007-Chapter-02-annexe-4-EN.pdf
[22] http://www.gunpolicy.org/firearms/region/australia
[23] http://library.med.utah.edu/WebPath/TUTORIAL/GUNS/GUNSTAT.html
[24] ABC Foreign Correspondent – Michael Brissenden March 2011
[25] Ibid
[26] ABC Foreign Correspondent – Michael Brissenden March 2011
[27] http://www.legalmatch.com/law-library/article/arizona-gun-laws.html
[28] Ibid
[29] http://en.wikipedia.org/wiki/Life,_liberty_and_the_pursuit_of_happiness
[30] Paul VI, Pope (1968) "Humanae Vitae" – Vatican - Archived from the original on 2011-03-18.
[31] http://www.zenit.org/article-13159?l=english
[32] Dig Deeper". Evangelical Lutheran Church in America
[33] Where does God stand on abortion – USA Today – 13 August 2006
[34] http://blogs.reuters.com/faithworld/2009/05/15/gallup-first-more-americans-now-pro-life-than-pro-choice/
[35] Ibid
[36] PEW Research Center – 21st July-5th August 2010

[37] Amnesty International "The Death Penalty in 2009" - Retrieved 29 May 2010

[38] http://en.wikipedia.org/wiki/List_of_country_legal_systems

[39] e.g. "After 21 Years in Prison - including 16 on Death Row - Curtis McCarty is Exonerated Based on DNA Evidence", The Innocence Project press release, May 11, 2007.

[40] Executed But Possibly Innocent" at Death Penalty Information Center.

[41] "Executing the Innocent", Northwestern Univ. School of Law Center on Wrongful Convictions

[42] http://www.deathpenaltyinfo.org/number-executions-state-and-region-1976

[43] http://www.guardian.co.uk/commentisfree/cifamerica/2012/jan/03/racial-bias-us-death-penalty

[44] Gallup Poll 5-8 May 2011

[45] Eubios Journal of Asian and International Bioethics 14 (2004), 214-216.

[46] Nero was not a fiddle player, but a lyre player (the fiddle was not invented for at least another 1500 years). Suetonius states Nero played the lyre while Rome burned, see Suetonius, The Lives of Twelve Caesars, Life of Nero 38; For a detailed explanation of this transition see M.F. Gyles "Nero Fiddled while Rome Burned", The Classical Journal (1948), pp. 211–217 – nevertheless, the idea that Nero played any kind of musical instrument is an urban legend, since he was away from Rome at the time of the fire

[47] Lydia Saad – Gallup.com, 30 March 2012

[48] Ibid

[49] http://tigger.uic.edu/~pdoran/012009_Doran_final.pdf

[50] Tim Wall – Discovery News, 14 Nov 2011

[51] Joshua Green – Bloomberg Businessweek, 30 May 2012

[52] Status of Ratification of the Kyoto Protocol". United Nations Framework Convention on Climate Change.

[53] Ibid

[54] David Ljunggren – Reuters - OTTAWA | Tue Dec 13, 2011

[55] Ibid

[56] The Politicization of Climate Change and Polarization in the American Public's Views of Global Warming – 2001-2010.- pp 159-160

[57] Ibid – p 160

[58] Ibid –p 160, Oreskes and Conway – 2010

[59] Ibid – p 180

[60] Cool dudes: the denial of climate change among conservative white males in the United States – McCright and Dunlap

[61] Bryan Walsh – Time Science, 04 October 2011

[62] http://www.law.cornell.edu/constitution/constitution.amendmentxiii.html

[63] "The Constitution: Amendments 11-27"

[64] Pepper, William (2003). An Act of State: The Execution of Martin Luther King. Verso. p. 159

[65] "Another Open Letter to Woodrow Wilson" W.E.B. DuBois, September, 1913

[66] http://en.wikipedia.org/wiki/Racial_segregation_in_the_United_States

[67] Williams, Donnie; Wayne Greenhaw (2005). The Thunder of Angels: The Montgomery Bus Boycott and the People who Broke the Back of Jim Crow. Chicago Review Press. p. 48.

[68] Montgomery Bus Boycott ~ Civil Rights Movement Veterans

[69] "Executive Order 9981". Harry S. Truman Library and Museum

[70] Strafication: A Biosocial Perspective". Du Bois Review: Social Science Research on Race

[71] Jackson, Kenneth T. Crabgrass Frontier: The Suburbanization of the United States. New York: Oxford University Press, 1985

[72] When Work Disappears: The World of the New Urban Poor By William Julius Wilson. 1996

[73] Jackson, Kenneth T. Crabgrass Frontier: The Suburbanization of the United States. New York: Oxford University Press, 1985

[74] Racial Discrimination and Redlining in Cities (PDF)

[75] Eisenhauer, Elizabeth (2001). "In poor health: Supermarket redlining and urban nutrition". GeoJournal 53 (2): 125–133.

[76] When Work Disappears: The World of the New Urban Poor By William Julius Wilson. 1996

[77] Kimberly N. Alleyne - America's Wire Staff, americaswire.org

[78] http://en.wikipedia.org/wiki/Rodney_King

[79] Ibid

[80] Theage.com.au, 4 July 2012

[81] Ibid

[82] Ibid

[83] Case-Shiller Housing price Index

[84] US Bureau of Labor Statistics

[85] US National Debt Clock

[86] Wall Street and the Financial Crisis: Anatomy of a Financial Collapse.

[87] Geithner speech – 9 June 2008

[88] FCIC Report-Conclusions Excerpt-January 2011

[89] http://www.relbanks.com/rankings/worlds-safest-banks

[90] The Short And Distort: Stock Manipulation In A Bear Market – Investopedia, 19 Jan 2009

[91] Wells Fargo Economic Research-Weekly Economic and Financial Commentary-17 September, 2010

[92] CSI: credit crunch". Economist.com. 2007-10-18

[93] Zakaria: A More Disciplined America | Newsweek Business | Newsweek.com

[94] Economist - A Helping Hand to Homeowners - Economist.com. 23 Oct 2008

[95] MBA Survey-Q3 2009". Mbaa.org. 2009-11-19

[96] David Eagleman in Incognito: The Secret Lives of the Brain

[97] The Subprime Mortgage Crisis Explained - Stock-market-investors.com.

[98] FCIC Report-Conclusions-January 2011

[99] Bank Systems & Technology". 2008

[100] Lynnley Browning (2007-03-27). "The Subprime Loan Machine". nytimes.com (New York City: Arthur Ochs Sulzberger, Jr.)

[101] Ben Steverman and David Bogoslaw (October 18, 2008). "The Financial Crisis Blame Game – BusinessWeek
[102] NYT-Reckoning-Profits Illusory, Bonuses Real
[103] Michael Simkovic, Competition and Crisis in Mortgage Securitization
[104] Ibid
[105] Demyanyk, Yuliya; Van Hemert, Otto (2008-08-19). "Understanding the Subprime Mortgage Crisis". Working Paper Series. Social Science Electronic Publishing.
[106] FCIC Report-Conclusion-January 2011
[107] FBI - Financial Crimes Report to the Public - Fiscal Years 2010-2011, (1/10/ 09 – 30/09/10)
[108] US House of Representatives Committee on Government Oversight and Reform (22 October 2008)
[109] SEC – Rating Agency Rules". Sec.gov. 03 Dec 2008
[110] Birger, Jon (6 August 2008). "The woman who called Wall Street's meltdown" Fortune.
[111] FCIC Final Report-Conclusions-January 2011
[112] Labaton, Stephen (27 Sept 2008). "SEC Concedes Oversight Flaws". The New York Times
[113] Michael Simkovic, "Competition and Crisis in Mortgage Securitization
[114] Ibid
[115] The Economist-Derivatives-A Nuclear Winter?
[116] Ibid
[117] Oil & Gas Journal, Vol 103, No 47, 19 Dec 2005
[118] Refer to Appendix C
[119] Rowena Mason – telegraph.co.uk – 22 March 2010
[120] http://emergingmoney.com/stocks/big-oil-moving-fast-to-get-ahead-of-peak-oil/
[121] https://www.citigroupgeo.com/pdf/SEUNHGJJ.pdf - 15 Feb 2012
[122] http://www.investorlinks.com/newsletters/1751/another-bakken-found/
[123] Kraushaar, Jack P., and Robert A. Ristinen. Energy and the Environment-2nd ed. New York, NY: Wiley & Sons Inc., 2006. 54–56.
[124] (PDF). Federal Register 76 (72): 21003–21005
[125] Hartnett-White, K. (2011)
[126] Associated Press – 27 October 2007
[127] Chemicals Used in Hydraulic Fracturing (Report). Committee on Energy and Commerce US House of Representatives. April 18, 2011
[128] US Department of Health and Human Services.
[129] Chemicals Used in Hydraulic Fracturing (Report). Committee on Energy and Commerce US House of Representatives. April 18, 2011
[130] Gadeken, Larry L., Halliburton Company (08-Nov-1989). Radioactive well logging method.
[131] Chemicals Used in Hydraulic Fracturing (Report). Committee on Energy and Commerce US House of Representatives. April 18, 2011
[132] Ibid
[133] Renee Lewis Kosnik, MSEL, JD Research Director, Oil and Gas Accountability Project

[134] Schmidt, Charles (1 August 2011). "Blind Rush? Shale Gas Boom Proceeds Amid Human Health Questions". Environmental Health Perspectives 119: a348-a353. DOI:10.1289/ehp.119-a348

[135] theForefront. Colorado School of Public Health. 19 March 2012

[136] Fact-Based Regulation for Environmental Protection in Shale Gas Development (Report). University of Texas at Austin. February 2012

[137] PG&E Hinkley Chromium Cleanup California Environmental Protection Agency, 9/10/08

[138] Jeremy P Jacobs of Greenwire New York Times, 18 August 2011

[139] Elliot Blair Smith, USA TODAY – 6 Feb 2006

[140] Ibid

[141] Ibid

[142] Elizabeth Bluemink (Thursday, June 10, 2010). "Size of Exxon spill remains disputed". Anchorage Daily News

[143] Brandon Keim (March 24, 2009). "The Exxon Valdez Spill Is All Around Us". Wired Science

[144] Warren Richey, Staff writer of The Christian Science Monitor /26 June, 2008

[145] Varma, Roli; Daya R. Varma (2005). "The Bhopal Disaster of 1984". Bulletin of Science, Technology and Society

[146] http://www.mp.gov.in/bgtrrdmp/relief.htm

[147] Eckerman I (2011) Bhopal Gas Catastrophe 1984: Causes and Consequences

[148] AK Dubey (21 June 2010). First14 News

[149] Eckerman I (2011) Bhopal Gas Catastrophe 1984: Causes and Consequences

[150] "Chronology". Bhopal Information Center, UCC. November 2006

[151] Leslie Kaufman – The New York Times, 10 December 2009

[152] ENS-Newswire 10 December 2009

[153] Chevron fined for Amazon pollution by Ecuador court. BBC News (BBC). 15 February 2011

[154] Patricia Hurtado and Bob Van Voris - May 15, 2012 - Bloomberg

[155] http://www.chevron.com/ecuador/background/

[156] Bowoto v. Chevron Texaco Corp., 312 F. Supp. 2d 1229 (N.D. Cal. 2004)

[157] Comments by American Chinese Medicine Association

[158] Ibid

[159] Ibid

[160] Ibid

[161] Ronald Ricker MD – Huffington Post

[162] Ibid

[163] UN International Narcotics Control Board (INCB) report - 2009

[164] Gary Gatyas – IMS Health, 6 October 2010

[165] Senators Who Weakened Drug Bill Got Millions From Industry, USA Today, May 10, 2007

[166] John LaMattina, Contributor - Former president of Pfizer R&D/senior partner at PureTech Ventures

[167] http://projects.propublica.org/docdollars/

[168] USATODAY.com - Drugmakers go farthest to sway Congress

[169] The West Australia, 3 July 2012

[170] Ibid
[171] Pharmaceutical market Group, 3 July 2012
[172] Jim Edwards – CBS Money Watch, 12 march 2010
[173] Ibid
[174] Ibid
[175] Jonathan Emord –The Rise of Tyranny, publisher – Sentinel Press
[176] Ibid
[177] Ibid
[178] Blaszczyk, R. L. (2008). Producing Fashion: Commerce, Culture and Consumers. Philadelphia: University of Pennsylvania Press
[179] Marchese, John. "A Rough Ride." The New York Times. 13 September 1992
[180] The Marlboro Man." AdAge.com. 26 February 2007
[181] Turning morons into millionaires, Herald-Journal
[182] Facts A La Carte." Whudafxup with Big Tobacco?. 2007. 28 February 2007
[183] http://www.cdc.gov/tobacco/data_statistics/fact_sheets/tobacco_industry/marketing/
[184] Center for Disease Control and prevention – Sept 2010
[185] Facts A La Carte." Whudafxup with Big Tobacco?. 2007. 28 February 2007
[186] Tobacco Advertising and Promotion." Greater Dallas Council on Alcohol & Drug Abuse. 2005 - 20 March 2007
[187] Global Smoking Statistics." About. 2007. 10 April 2007
[188] Ibid
[189] Brian Hartman – ABC News, 7 Sept 2010
[190] Ibid
[191] Ibid
[192] Brian Ross – ABC News Video 17 November 2009
[193] http://www.tobaccofreekids.org/
[194] Brian Hartman – ABC News, 7 Sept 2010
[195] Ibid
[196] National Obesity Trends, CDC NCHS, 2010
[197] Early Release of Selected Estimates Based on Data From the 2004 National Health Interview Survey, CDC NCHS, 2005-06-21
[198] Childhood Overweight and Obesity – cdc.gov
[199] Thomson Reuters – 30 April 2012
[200] http://www.cdc.gov/obesity/adult/causes/index.html
[201] CBS News – 11 Feb 2009
[202] Ibid
[203] Melanie Hicken - Business Insider, January 28, 2012
[204] Jeannine Stein, Los Angeles Times, 22 December 2011
[205] Rudd Center for Food Policy & Obesity at Yale
[206] Bowman et al. (2004)
[207] Eating up the Amazon – Greenpeace, 6 April 2006
[208] Fast Food Nation, Eric Schlosser – Penguin Books, 2002
[209] Greenpeace – 17 June 2008
[210] That Burger You're Eating is Mostly Corn - Scientific American, 12 Nov 2008
[211] Bob Lawrence – director of the Center for a Liveable Future, Johns Hopkins Bloomberg School of Public Health

[212] Ibid
[213] Dogwood Alliance
[214] Ibid
[215] http://www.treehugger.com/culture/no-free-refills-fast-food-packaging-industry-destroying-southern-us-forests.html
[216] Norman Braksick, president of Asgrow Seed Co., a subsidiary of Monsanto, quoted in the Kansas City Star, March 7, 1994
[217] Phil Angell, Monsanto's director of corporate communications, quoted in the New York Times, October 25, 1998
[218] http://organicconsumers.org/monsanto/index.cfm
[219] Vermont Public Radio – 5 May 2012
[220] Sustainable Business – 1 May 2012
[221] http://www.percyschmeiser.com/conflict.htm
[222] Ibid
[223] CropChoice News – 21 May 2001
[224] NaturalSociety - February 27, 2012
[225] Ibid
[226] Ibid
[227] Pellow, David N. Resisting Global Toxics: Transnational Movements for Environmental Justice
[228] York, Geoffrey; Mick, Hayley; "Last Ghost of the Vietnam War", The Globe and Mail, July 12, 2008
[229] Fawthrop, Tom (November 4, 2004). "Agent Orange Victims Sue Monsanto". CorpWatch.
[230] http://en.wikipedia.org/wiki/Agent_Orange#cite_note-59
[231] Published on Tuesday, February 7, 2012 by Common Dreams
[232] Charlotte P. Brennand, PhD, Extension Food Safety Specialist. "Bovine Somatotropin in Milk
[233] Samuel S. Epstein, M.D., Professor Environmental Medicine, University of Illinois Chicago, School of Public Health:
[234] Wickenheiser, M (2003-07-08). "Oakhurst Sued by Monsanto Over Milk Advertising". Portland Press Herald
[235] Safeway milk free of bovine hormone". Seattle Post-Intelligencer. Associated Press. 2007-01-22
[236] All US Company-Operated Stores Use Dairy Sourced Without the Use of rBGH". Starbucks Corporation
[237] Kroger to complete transition to certified rBST-free milk by early 2008 (press release). Kroger. 2007
[238] Rudel, R A, Seryak, L M, and Brody, J G (2008)
[239] Contamination of rice bran oil with PCB used as the heating medium by leakage through penetration holes at the heating coil tube in deodorization chamber. Hatamura Institute for the Advancement of Technology
[240] Staff Profile:Dr Philippa Darbre
[241] Michael Grunwald –Staff Writer, Washing Post – 1 January 2002 in an article entitled "Monsanto hid decades of pollution"
[242] Denzel Ferguson – Mississippi State University biologist

[243] Ibid

[244] Ibid

[245] Michael Grunwald – Washington Post, 1 January 2002

[246] http://www.epa.gov/oecaagct/ag101/cropmajor.html

[247] http://www.epa.gov/oecaagct/tpes.html

[248] The Quality of our nation's waters: Pesticides in the nation's streams and ground water, 1992–2001. Chapter 1, Page 4. US Geological Survey

[249] Miller GT (2004), Sustaining the Earth, 6th edition. Thompson Learning, Inc. Pacific Grove, California. Chapter 9, Pages 211-216.

[250] Ibid

[251] Ibid

[252] Pesticide Data Program (February 2006) Annual Summary Calendar Year 2005

[253] PANNA PDF – May 2004

[254] Ibid

[255] Fields of Peril; Child Labor in US Agriculture - Zama Coursen-Neff, deputy director of the Children's Rights Division at Human Rights Watch

[256] Ibid

[257] Ibid

[258] Ibid

[259] http://www.hrw.org/news/2010/05/05/us-child-farmworkers-dangerous-lives

[260] Worst Forms of Child Labor Convention of the International Labor Organization

[261] Zama Coursen-Neff – The Hill – 7 May 2012

[262] http://www.libraryindex.com/pages/2170/Farm-Animals-FACTORY-FARMING.html

[263] Ibid

[264] Public health implications of meat production and consumption

[265] "Factory Farming: The Impact of Animal Feeding Operations on the Environment and Health of Local Communities"

[266] Miller GT (2004), Sustaining the Earth, 6th edition. Thompson Learning, Inc. Pacific Grove, California. Chapter 9, Pages 211–216.

[267] "Concentrated animal feeding operations", Centers for Disease Control and Prevention, United States Department of Health and Human Services.

[268] Ibid

[269] http://www.sciencedaily.com/releases/2011/04/110415083153.htm

[270] Ibid

[271] US Department of Agriculture - Agricultural Research Service, 5 June, pp. 37–44).

[272] Kaufmann, Marc. "Largest Pork Processor to Phase Out Crates", The Washington Post, 26 January, 2007.

[273] Ibid

[274] Compassion in World Farming – Animal health and disease

[275] http://science.nationalgeographic.com/science/health-and-human-body/human-body/food-safety.html#page=1

[276] Housing, space, feed and water United Egg Producers

[277] Sherwin, C.M., Richards, G.J and Nicol, C.J. 2010. Comparison of the welfare of layer hens in 4 housing systems in the UK. British Poultry Science, 51(4): 488-499

[278] Institute of Science, Technology and Public Policy Maharishi University of Management

[279] Environmental Integrity Project, September 2010

[280] Water Sentinels: Factory Farms - Sierra Club

[281] Most US Antibiotics Fed to Healthy Livestock - Kristin Leutwyler – Scientific American, 10 Jan 2001

[282] Joint WHO/FAO/OIE Expert Workshop on Non-human Antimicrobial Usage and Antimicrobial Resistance Geneva, 1 – 5 December 2003

[283] Wall Street Journal, "Pennsylvania Finds High Toll in Hospital-Acquired Infections," July 13, 2005, p. D4.

[284] Amy Silverstein – Global Post, 23 march 2012

[285] Suzi Frazer – aquafeed.com, 23 Dec 2005

[286] http://www.sierraclub.org/watersentinels/factoryfarms.aspx

[287] David Wessel – Wall Street Journal, 19 April 2011

[288] Ibid

[289] Offshoring: Is It a Win-Win Game?" Diana Farrell, McKinsey Global Institute, August 2003.

[290] Daniel T. Griswold and Dale Buss, http://www.mackinac.org/6821 - 15 Sept 2004

[291] Washington Post – 12 August 2011

[292] Ibid

[293] Sean John Setisa Report". National Labor Committee – October 2003

[294] Ibid

[295] Sage, George H. (1999). "Justice Do It! The Nike Transnational Advocacy Network: Organization, Collective Actions, and Outcomes". Sociology of Sport Journal 16: 206-235.

[296] Nike Annual SEC income statement

[297] Sweating for Fashion – The Economist – 4 March 2004

[298] "Foxconn Plans To Increase China Workforce to 1.3 Million". Focus Taiwan News Channel. 2010-8-19

[299] "The Forbidden City of Terry Gou". The Wall Street Journal. 2007-08-11

[300] "Apple hit by China Foxconn factory report". BBC. 2012-03-30

[301] Charles Duhigg, David Barboza – theage.com.au – 1 Feb 2012

[302] Ibid

[303] New York Times interview with Li Mingqi, 26 Jan 2012

[304] Ibid

[305] Julianne Pepitone - CNN Money – 29 March 2012

[306] Ibid

[307] Ibid

[308] John Vausse – CNN, 2 June 2010

[309] http://www.apple.com/supplierresponsibility/code-of-conduct/

[310] CBS News – 27 Jan 2012

[311] Poornima Gupta and Edwin Chan - Reuters, San Francisco, Thu Mar 29, 2012

[312] Source – New York Times

[313] The Age – Business Day – 29 Oct 2011

[314] Saul Eslake, Program Director with the Grattan Institute

[315] Lynn Stout – National Times, Political Opinion – 29 November 2011

[316] http://en.wikipedia.org/wiki/US_Airways

[317] Mark A. Hofmann – Business Insurance, 22 April 2005

[318] David Koenig, AP Airlines Writer | Associated Press – Fri, Apr 27, 2012

[319] Chris Isidore, CNN/Money senior writer, 15 September 2005

[320] Aero-News Network

[321] Forbes.com

[322] Aero-News Network

[323] Star – Telegram 15 Dec 2011

[324] Michael Lindsay – New York Times – 30 Nov 2011

[325] Labaton, Stephen (October 3, 2008). "Agency's '04 Rule Let Banks Pile Up New Debt, and Risk". The New York Times

[326] Ibid

[327] New York Times – Dealbook, 7 March 2008

[328] Simon Bowers - guardian.co.uk, 17 October 2008

[329] Wall Street Journal – 18 December 2009

[330] Ben Levisohn – Bloomberg Business week 3/19/2008

[331] Walter Hamilton, Jim Puzzanghera and Andrew Tangel, Los Angeles Times – 27 April 2012

[332] Wall Street Bankers in line for $70bn payout

[333] Christopher Helman – Forbes.com

[334] Mark Colvan – ABC Radio, 15 May 2012

[335] http://en.wikipedia.org/wiki/Hedge_fund

[336] Ineichen, Alexander (2002). Absolute Returns: the risks and opportunities of hedge fund investing. John Wiley & Sons. pp. 441–4. ISBN 0-471-25120-8.

[337] Top hedge fund earners – Institutional Investor, Alpha Magazine

[338] Louise Story – The New York Times, 24 March 2009

[339] Ed Pilkington – The Guardian, 10 march 2011

[340] http://www.pinoymoneytalk.com/category/richest-people/

[341] http://topics.bloomberg.com/bloomberg-billionaires-index/

[342] en.wikipedia.org/wiki/The_Giving_Pledge

[343] http://www.huffingtonpost.com/2012/04/20/giving-pledge-warren-buffett-bill-gates_n_1441387.html

[344] Ibid

[345] http://givingpledge.org/.

[346] Rule of 72 states that if you divide 72 by the annual growth rate, the result will be the length of time it takes for the growth to double

[347] Food and Agricultural Organization of the United Nations – 25 March 2010

[348] Anthony Faiola - Washington Post Staff Writer, Friday, October 10, 2008

[349] Ibid

[350] Ibid

[351] Paul B. Farrell – World News Daily, 23 Feb 2010

[352] Ibid

[353] Hansard, 11 Dec 1947

[354] Ibid

[355] Haretz.com – 6 December 2011

[356] Lenczowski, George (1990). American Presidents and the Middle East. Duke University Press. pp. 157.

[357] Quigley, John B. (1990). Palestine and Israel: a challenge to justice. Duke University Press. pp. 37.

[358] Before & after: US foreign policy and the 11 September crisis By Phyllis Benn

[359] http://en.wikipedia.org/wiki/State_of_Palestine

[360] Guy Azriel, CNN, April 24, 2012

[361] http://unispal.un.org/pdfs/OCHA_IsrSettlementPolicies.pdf

[362] US State Department - UN

[363] http://www.jewishvirtuallibrary.org/jsource/UN/usvetoes.html

[364] John J. Mearsheimer and Stephen M. Walt "The Israel Lobby and US Foreign Policy"

[365] Steve Jones - US Foreign Policy Guide

[366] http://www.vaughns-1-pagers.com/politics/us-foreign-aid.htm

[367] Truman, Year of Decisions: 1945, p. 207

[368] Richard Salsman, Forbes.com 26 June 2011

[369] https://www.cia.gov/news-information/speeches/

[370] Boose, Donald W. (Winter 1995–96). Portentous Sideshow: The Korean Occupation Decision. . Parameters: US Army War College Quarterly (US Army War College) 5 (4): 112–129. OCLC 227845188

[371] http://en.wikipedia.org/wiki/Korean_War

[372] Rhem, Kathleen T. (8 June 2000). "Defense.gov News Article: Korean War Death Stats Highlight Modern DoD Safety Record". defense.gov. US Department of Defense. Retrieved 22 December 2011.

[373] http://en.wikipedia.org/wiki/Korean_War#Casualties

[374] http://www.vietnamgear.com/Indochina1950.aspx

[375] http://en.wikipedia.org/wiki/Role_of_the_United_States_in_the_Vietnam_War

[376] Ibid

[377] Ibid

[378] http://faculty.smu.edu/dsimon/Change-Viet.html

[379] American War and Military Operations Casualties: Lists and Statistics

[380] Rummel, R.J (1997), "Table 6.1A. Vietnam Democide : Estimates, Sources, and Calculations,

[381] Philip Sheldon. 20 Years After Victory, April 1995, Folder 14, Box 24, Douglas Pike Collection: Unit 06 - Democratic Republic of Vietnam, The Vietnam Archive, Texas Tech University.

[382] Ibid

[383] http://en.wikipedia.org/wiki/War_in_Afghanistan_(2001-present)

[384] War in Afghanistan – 2001-present

[385] United Nations Assistance Mission in Afghanistan

[386] Cost of Iraq, Afghanistan and Anti-Terrorism Operations: - Journalist's Resource.org.

[387] Poll: Talk First, Fight Later". CBS.com, 24 Jan. 2003.

[388] According to the French academic Dominique Reynié

[389] Burkeman, Oliver (21 November 2003). "Invasion right but 'illegal', says US hawk". The Age (Melbourne)

[390] http://www.theage.com.au – 3rd January 2012

[391] Joseph E. Stiglitz and Linda J. Bilmes – Washington Post, Sunday, September 5, 2010
[392] United Nations Treaty Collection: Convention against Torture and Other Cruel, Inhuman or Degrading Treatment or Punishment
[393] Ibid
[394] Convention against Torture: article 1.1
[395] Dana Priest and Barton Gellman - Washington Post - Thursday, December 26, 2002
[396] Rajiv Chandrasekaran and Peter Finn - Washington Post Foreign Service, Mar 11, 2002
[397] Dana Priest - Washington Post - January 2, 2005; http://www.pulitzer.org/archives/6962
[398] Dana Priest and Barton Gellman - Washington Post - Thursday, December 26, 2002
[399] History of an Interrogation Technique: Water Boarding". World News with Charles Gibson (ABC News). 2005-11-29
[400] Thomas M. Defrank / DAILY NEWS WASHINGTON BUREAU CHIEF, June 1, 2009
[401] CBS News "McCain: Japanese Hanged For Waterboarding", CBS News, 29 November 2007, accessed 9 November 2010.
[402] Pappas, Alex (September 24, 2010). "Herman Cain, former Godfather's Pizza CEO, is contemplating 2012 run". The Daily Caller
[403] The Hill, July 5, 2010
[404] Fiscal Times, September 12, 2010
[405] The Hill, July 5, 2010
[406] The New York Times (Washington DC) www.nytimes.com/2010/03/14/weekinreview/14Iliptak.html
[407] Przybyla, Heidi (March 26, 2010). "Tea Party Advocates Who Scorn Socialism Want a Government Job". Bloomberg News
[408] http://www.teapartytribune.com/2012/03/20/the-morality-of-free-market-capitalism/
[409] http://www.firearmstruth.com/2012/national-rifle-association-diminishing-the-constitution
[410] This includes homicides, suicides and accidental deaths
[411] EG Krug, KE Powell and LL Dahlberg. "Firearm-related deaths in the United States and 35 other high- and upper-middle-income countries"- International Journal of Epidemiology 1998:27:214-221.
[412] http://www.forbes.com/2010/03/18/tea-party-ignorant-taxes-opinions-columnists-bruce-bartlett.html
[413] Ibid
[414] Ibid
[415] Combined surveys from November 2010 through February 2011
[416] wd4freedom 18 October 2009
[417] drawn from the work of economist Edward N. Wolff at New York University (2010).
[418] Survey conducted by Michael I Norton of Harvard Business School and Dan Ariely of Duke University
[419] OECD – Sweden ranked 3rd behind Australia and Canada. United States ranked 7th.
[420] IMF – September 2011

[421] Forbes.com 2010
[422] USA Today – 12 September 2010
[423] http://www.policymic.com/articles/3250/sweden-s-socialist-based-society-can-be-a-model-for-america
[424] http://elections.nytimes.com/2012/campaign-finance
[425] Liptak, Adam (2010-01-21). "Justices, 5–4, Reject Corporate Spending Limit". New York Times.
[426] Anthony DiClemente - Barclays Capital analyst – 31 Jan 2012
[427] Ibid
[428] Jim Snyder – Bloomberg News – 24 Feb 2011
[429] Ibid
[430] Ibid
[431] Corruption Perception Index 2011
[432] The Smoking Gun Tape (Transcript of the recording of a meeting between President Nixon and H. R. Haldeman). Watergate.info website. June 23, 1972
[433] http://en.wikipedia.org/wiki/Watergate_scandal
[434] White (1975), Breach of Faith, p. 29. "And the most punishing blow of all was to come in late afternoon when the President received, in his Oval Office, the Congressional leaders of his party — Barry Goldwater, Hugh Scott and John Rhodes. The accounts of all three coincide… Goldwater averred that there were not more than fifteen votes left in his support in the Senate…."
[435] Ibid
[436] Annual report - American Civil Liberties Union, Volume 5
[437] US Department of the Treasury. (2011) "History of 'In God We Trust
[438] The US National Mottos: Their History and Constitutionality, ReligiousTolerance.org
[439] Atheist protests 'In God We Trust' posting
[440] LYNCH v. DONNELLY, 465 US 668 (1984) US Supreme Court
[441] David Swnason – Centre for Research on Globalization
[442] Sheryl gay Stolberg, New York Times – 12 march 2008
[443] Doyle McManus – Los Angeles Times, 5 June 2011
[444] Ibid
[445] Alexander Eichler – Huffington Post, 29 Dec 2011
[446] 2011 Legatum Prosperity Index – Forbes.com
[447] Schecter, Jerrold L.; Deriabin, Peter S. (1992). The Spy Who Saved the World: How a Soviet Colonel Changed the Course of the Cold War. Scribner.
[448] http://www.history.com/this-day-in-history.do?
[449] Ibid
[450] Frum, David (2000). How We Got Here: The '70s. New York, New York: Basic Books. pp. 49–51.
[451] https://www.cia.gov/offices-of-cia/clandestine-service/code-of-ethics.html
[452] Stockwell, John (October 1987). "The Secret Wars of the CIA, a lecture".
[453] David Ignatius – Quad-City Times, 31 May 2012
[454] Ibid
[455] Daily Mail UK, 19 June 2012
[456] Paul Harris – The Guardian, 5 June 2012

[457] Michael Isikoff – NBC News, 30 April 2012
[458] Ibid
[459] Ibid
[460] Gary D. Solis (2010). The Law of Armed Conflict: International Humanitarian Law in War. Cambridge University Press.
[461] Targeted killing is a necessary option, Sofaer, Abraham D., Hoover Institution, 26 March, 2004
[462] www.aclu.org/national-security/frequently-asked-questions-about-targeting-killing
[463] Public Law Pub.L. 107-56
[464] Grayden Carter – What We've Lost, p92, 2004
[465] Surveillance Under the USA PATRIOT Act, UCLA, 10 Dec 2010
[466] Ibid
[467] EFF analysis of the provisions of the USA PATRIOT Act that relate to online activities, "Were our Freedoms the Problem?"
[468] http://www.crf-usa.org/america-responds-to-terrorism/the-patriot-act.html
[469] American Library Association, Resolution on the USA PATRIOT Act and Libraries
[470] http://www.crf-usa.org/america-responds-to-terrorism/the-patriot-act.html
[471] www.ethicapublishing.com/ethical/3CH7.pdf
[472] https://wwws.whitehouse.gov/petitions/!/petition/repeal-patriot-act/JF1pdPKg
[473] Linus Atarah – Other News, 20 April 2012
[474] Ibid
[475] Victor David Hanson – National Review Online, 2 June 2011
[476] http://en.wikipedia.org/wiki/Federal_judicial_appointment_history
[477] The Eighth United Nations Survey on Crime Trends and the Operations of Criminal Justice Systems (2002) (United Nations Office on Drugs and Crime, Centre for International Crime Prevention)
[478] Boston.com – business updates, 21 May 2012
[479] Ibid
[480] Huffington Post – 27 March 2012
[481] Amy Goodman & Juan González – Democracy Now, 22 Jan 2010
[482] Ed Hoernick – CNN Politics, 6 November 2008
[483] Ibid
[484] Grayden Carter – What We've Lost, p 204
[485] Ibid pp 208-9
[486] Ibid p 281
[487] Ibid p 320
[488] National Obesity Trends, CDC NCHS, 2010
[489] http://www.icta.org/global-warming-and-the-environment/global-warming-air-pollution/
[490] Eisenhower's Farewell Address to the Nation – 17th January 1961
[491] PERPETUAL WAR FOR PERPETUAL PEACE: How We Got to Be So Hated - 2002 by Gore Vidal
[492] Ibid p14
[493] Peter Hartcher – Spoilt West invites its own decline, theage.com.au 12 June 2012

www.ingramcontent.com/pod-product-compliance
Lightning Source LLC
Chambersburg PA
CBHW030303290526
45785CB00001B/192